C000148357

DURH

ESSAYS ON
SENSE OF PLACE

Douglas Pocock

Durham: City of Durham Trust

First published 1999 by
City of Durham Trust

Printed by Macdonald Press, Ltd., Spennymoor
Typeset at ULCC

ISBN 0 902776 05 3

Contents

Illustrations

Preface and Acknowledgements

The aim of this volume is to share with the reader some of the qualities of a city which medieval writers likened to Jerusalem, which Ruskin termed among the wonders of the world, and which Pevsner, more modestly, called one of the architectural experiences of Europe. It is the outcome of an acquaintance spanning a quarter of a century, during which I have had the privilege to live and work in, and care for, the city. During this time the focus of my research from within the University Department of Geography has often overlapped work as secretary of the local civic society, the City of Durham Trust. From this joint venture I have selected nine essays which, it is hoped, will convey in coherent sequence aspects of the city's unique sense of place.

Three of the essays, chapters 4, 7 and 8, are adapted from articles which originally appeared in the *Transactions of the Institute of British Geographers*, namely, 'Some characteristics of mental maps: an empirical study,' NS1 (1976), 493-512; 'Valued landscape and memory: the view from Prebends' Bridge,' NS7 (1982), 354-64; 'Place evocation: the Galilee Chapel in Durham Cathedral,' NS21, (1996) 379-86. The quotations from the poems, 'Going, Going' by Philip Larkin, from *Collected Poems by Philip Larkin* (1988) and 'Four Quartets' by T.S. Eliot, from *Collected Poems 1909-1962* by T.S. Eliot (1963), also the poem, 'Durham', from *A Choice of Anglo-Saxon Verse* by Richard Hamer (1970), are all published by kind permission of Faber and Faber Ltd.

Most of the photographs, including the front cover, are from my own camera. Among the wider range of illustrations, I acknowledge with gratitude the permission to publish copyright material in the following Figures: 7- Master of University College; 8- Dean and Chapter of Durham; 12- The National Gallery of Scotland, Edinburgh; 13- V. & A. Picture Library; 14- © Copyright The British Museum; 15- Staatsbibliothek zu Berlin, Preussischer Kulturbesitz, Musikabteilung mit Mendelssohn-Archiv; 43- Ellen Ives; 44- Malcolm Thurlby; 52,53- Michelle Johnson. I am especially indebted to Michelle Johnson for preparation of the artwork, David Hume and Steven Allan for the cartography and Lisa Tempest for preparing the text; each has shown a professionalism befitting the subject of this volume.

1   Durham Distilled: The Quality of 'Durhamness'

In attempting to explicate the quality of 'Durhamness' I bring an outsider's curiosity and insider's love, together with a particular disciplinary training. My aim is to try and articulate that which the native-born already knows but may not be able – or see the need – to put into words, at the same time suggesting what Durham is saying to us, thereby reversing the normal process. Forgive the arrogance and naivety in this approach.

What, then, is Durham? In summary, it is an aesthetic high, an architectural innovation, a cultural benchmark. Durham is a visual delight, attractive from a great variety of angles, but notable above all for its great views which have been captured by artists and confirmed by scholars from the late middle ages to the modern day. Durham is also where the structural thrust problem in major buildings was resolved, where the rib-vault, buttress and pointed arch of the Gothic were first demonstrated. Again, Durham is the nation's monument to the Norman invasion, the last invasion of our country. It is little wonder, therefore, that in recent times the city should receive official ranking or statutory listing: its Conservation Area was early recognised and classed as 'outstanding', it is on the select list of National Heritage Towns drawn up by the British Council of Archaeology, and it is a UNESCO World Heritage Site.

The city is a physical manifestation of a significant event in our history – confirmation by the Normans of a site chosen for, or by, the North's most famous saint. It is a physical manifestation of a story, a story with a quality of legend concerning St. Cuthbert. Moreover, history and story have been certified for us in writings, verse and painting. (No landscape, it may be held, is truly rich until it has been certified in this manner, and is particularly so when the story has the quality of legend or myth). In consequence, Durham is assuredly somewhere, and the person from somewhere feels someone. As a place with identity, it reinforces our identity.

The distinctiveness of Durham's identity is associated with the fact that surprise infuses the key constituent elements. Size may well be the first element to call forth surprise, for if the cathedral has been taken as the touchstone of size, then one is certainly expecting something much bigger. The cathedral bestows the appellation 'city' to the settlement, but the urban form and accompanying facilities are surprisingly modest. Boundedness is a related, second element. The city is a distinct entity; it is not frayed at the edges; it does not stutter into being through suburbia (Figures 1-4). Given the speed of modern travel, it is almost possible to believe that town and country meet at a line as abrupt as in medieval times. The cathedral, as a marker, may initially beckon from afar – perhaps 8 to 10 miles distant – but it is then hidden until the last minute as one reaches or breaches the rim of the basin in which it is set.

The monumental climax is a highly distinctive element. Upstanding and outstanding, the cathedral is the tallest, grandest building on the highest site. Nature formed the peninsula, the 'hill-island' from which Durham derives its name, rising 100 feet above the encircling river, and man exploited the potential by raising a stone monument from the rocky pedestal by at least an equivalent height (Figures 5-6). It is a crowning, dramatic climax. On arrival, the visitor is no doubt that there is a there, there. For the community it is also the social anchor point, the focus of celebration for a myriad of diverse gatherings.

The townscape is in complete contrast to the climax, being domestic in scale, organic in layout and varied in age. It rises and falls, winds and staggers as if in sympathy with river course and topography. There is a coherence and legibility, but not one of instant revelation, for that way boredom lies. Rather, it is a richer experience, one which comes with effort, from following a series of intriguing beckonings, aided all the time by the changing silhouette of the architectural climax.

Greenness is a final, all-pervading quality. This consists of more than the regulatory provision of open space, urbanised manicured parkland or tree-lined streets. The countryside, even the working countryside, approaches and appears to enter the heart of the city. The views from all compass points illustrate this – from Old Durham, Shincliffe, Mount Joy, Windmill Hill, Observatory Hill, Flass Vale, Kepier. Cornfields may approach to within a quarter of a mile of the peninsula. Even closer are St. Margaret's Allotments, off leafy Margery Lane with the cathedral rising behind. The particular view here is Durham's equivalent of Constable's Salisbury cathedral from the water meadows. The contrast in terms of aesthetics and social worlds is surprising only to outsiders; for insiders it is part of the accepted order: part of Durham. We may also be aware of the symbolic value of the allotment site, for as our faith tells us we originated in a garden, so did our cathedral originate from stone dug in this garden. (Marked on some early maps as the 'Abbey Fishpond', the bowl-shape configuration betrays its original role as a quarry).

Not the least contribution to the greenness of Durham is the broad wedge which accompanies the river on its entire course through the city. The well-known view from Prebends' Bridge may be cited in this respect, not to admire the cathedral rising from the banks of trees, but to reflect that from the bridge one is looking towards the heart of the city and, at the same time, able to see the countryside beyond! It is a characteristic that from many parts of the middle of the city one can lift up one's eyes and see, not only the cathedral, but the rim with its green skyline.

The various elements together combine to constitute the quality of 'Durhamness'. The distinctiveness – the surprising distinctiveness – however, derives not only from the heightened degree to which elements are present, but from the co-existence of opposing qualities. A series of dualities, holding in tension two opposites, can be recognised. Thus Durham is spiritual and secular. It has at its heart cathedral and castle. Even the cathedral itself, in Sir Walter Scott's well-known words, is 'Half church of God, half castle 'gainst the Scot'.[1] Again, Durham is nature and culture. It is town and country. 'Town and country must be married,' wrote Ebenezer Howard a century ago. Here the marriage does not consist of thousands of units, each in its own green plot, as in his 'Garden Cities', but, rather, consists of a city in a garden: a large temple in the middle of greenery.

Fig. 1 View of Durham from east, near Sherburn Hospital.

Fig. 2 View of Durham from north, near Frankland Farm.

Fig. 3 View of Durham from south, from Windmill Hill.

Fig. 4 View of Durham from south-west, from Observatory Hill.

Fig. 5 View from Railway Station.

Fig. 6 View from below Framwellgate Bridge.

Durham is also monumentalism and the domestic. It speaks of master masons with international ideas and of more modest craftsmen and the vernacular. Durham is committed to one time period, yet is timeless in what it proclaims. As the capital of the county, it belongs to the folk of the county, who have considerable pride in their town: they/we are Cuthbert's people. Yet, Durham belongs to British history, western civilisation, the whole of Christendom. A series of paradoxes describes our city, then – a not inappropriate conclusion for a city which has a paradox enshrined at its centre: Cuthbert, a hermit and contemplative by inclination who drew to himself people and preferment.

All places are unique in terms of physical disposition and special in terms of human association. Durham, it is suggested, is particularly distinctive. Historically, it is as if people listened to what the landscape was saying and built accordingly. The landscape of the central hill-island in a basin with its rim of - seven? - hills has been claimed by feelings over the centuries. In the last fifty years planners have continued to listen to what the landscape was saying, though they have expressed it technically in terms of intervisibility and of sight-lines to and from the cathedral. To retain the uniqueness, this quality of Durhamness, there is a need to continue to listen and to respect what the ancients called the genius loci and what townscape analyst George Cullen has more recently termed 'the secret language of site'. The canvas of Durham was not, and is not, blank or abstract space on which the forces of economics and politics have free play for their brush work or designs.

This is the first time that economics and politics have been mentioned, even though environmental experience and spirit of place are anchored in these fields. Recently there have been moves towards a 'greening' of economics and politics. While I have reservations over the appropriateness of such techniques for the environment as discussed here, the key principal of 'sustainable development', whereby the needs of the present should not be satisfied at the expense of future generations, can be broadly applied. Quite simply, if the resource here is Durham, then sustainable development is that which does not compromise the quality of 'Durhamness'. Moreover, before considering individual proposals and any Environmental Impact Assessment, there is need to stop, reflect and query at a fundamental level whether the key agents of change are responding to demand or generating it. For instance, British Rail trebled the size of its car park ahead of electrification. Is this responding to, or stimulating demand? Again, housebuilders, and nationally-linked estate agents, press ever more forcefully for building land, while at the same time advertising sites as suitable for commuters to Tyneside and Teesside and, now, the south. Is this responding to demand, or generating it? When local and county authorities produce a strategy to boost tourism by ten per cent per annum, is that response or stimulation? And so on.

The same fundamental overview would also query whether over-concentration in the old city or centre is necessary or desirable, given modern transport and communications and given the political reality of Durham District and County. (The extent of over-concentration is evident from the number of planning applications – and proposals that do not reach that stage – which cover practically every open space, regardless of its designated use in the Local Plan).

The concept of sustainable development implies a holistic or contextual approach: of putting into context any development proposal, whatever its origin. This is not an excuse for a city-wide N.I.M.B.Y. Neither is it a recipe for a progressively fake historical place cut off from the flow of culture, little better than themed fantasy lands. It is readily acknowledged that history is essentially a flow. It is evident, for example, that the townscape of this 'timeless' city has changed – and often for the better. But in the context of its region, Durham did not share in the nineteenth-century industrial growth – and for good reasons. Neither has it been at the forefront of recent retail development – again for good reasons. Care must therefore be taken before any perceived catching-up operation is mooted. In particular, care must be taken over exploiting its potential for tourism, office development, high tech activities or as a dormitory settlement. Care is needed, since it will take very few generations of successful developments – each income-generating and job-creating, each perhaps desirable in its own right – before a small city becomes a metropolis, before Durham possesses the standard, the normal, the usual, the expected, but Durham is not a city of the expected. I am reminded of the pessimism in Philip Larkin's poem, 'Going, going', if Durham is substituted for England:

> Despite all the land left free,
> For the first time I feel somehow
> That it isn't going to last
> … And that will be Durham gone.[2]

I prefer the vision of T.S. Eliot, again with the same substitution:

> Here, the intersection of the timeless moment
> Is Durham and nowhere. Never and always.[3]

That is a paradox, but, as I have tried to show, Durham is a paradox.

2   Durham Observed: The Comment of Artist and Traveller

'I have no more noble city in all my realm.' This reported comment by Henry VI after a visit to Durham in 1448 has been echoed by a succession of visitors, be they travellers or diarists, antiquaries or topographers, authorities or artists. All have been attracted by the dramatic and distinctive appearance of the city. Their subsequent word or picture has heightened expectation, enriched experience and sustained memory. In so doing, their comments have not only preserved, but contributed to, perhaps even created, the city's perceived quality of place.

The unique combination of water, rock and building has been a feature of recorded observation since the very first description of the city in the early twelfth century.

> This city is renowned throughout all Britain,
> set on steep slopes and marvellously built with
> rocks all round. A strongly running river
> flows past enclosed by weirs.[1]

This earliest description, probably composed in the monastery at Durham, constitutes the country's last extant Old English or Anglo-Saxon poem. The evident pride of place was repeated in a much longer composition, in Latin, a mere fifty years later by a Durham monk, Brother Laurence. It has a similar opening:

> The ground rises up on high, a rocky plateau
> with rugged sides: sloping steeply in all
> directions it discourages an enemy, and moated by
> the river it mocks hostile forces. The rapid
> river envelops it in the shape of a horse-shoe,
> a watery vale encircles the lofty place.[2]

Visits by Leland (1530s), Camden (1580) and Speede (1610) have bequeathed us descriptions of the medieval city. But gone is the colour and feeling of the early poems; rather are they medieval gazetteers or directories giving a straight-forward structural outline – verbal descriptions, in fact, of details given on the earliest map of the city by Matthew Patterson. The only colour is in their antiquarian pursuit of legend or rumour. Thus Leland speculates on the narrow neck of the peninsula and the curious loop of the Wear.

> ... some hold opinion, that of ancient tyme, Were ran from the
> place wher now Elvet bridge is, straite down by St. Nicholas,
> now standing on a hille; and that the other course, part for
> policy, and part by digging of stones for building of the towne
> and minstre, was made a valley, and so the water course was
> conveyed that way, but I approve not full this conjecture.[3]

By the time of Celia Fiennes (1698) and Defoe (1724) we have diarists who evaluate as well as record. Thus, the former:

> I must say of the whole Citty of Durham its the noblest, cleane and pleasant buildings, streets large well pitched.[4]

Defoe observes:

> Durham is a little compact neatly contriv'd city, surrounded almost with the river Wear, which with the castle standing on an eminence, encloses the city in the middle of it; as the castle does also the cathedral, the bishop's palace, and the fine houses of the clergy, where they live in all the magnificence and splendour imaginable ... The town is well built but old.[5]

Appeals to the spiritual dimension of place were also evoked by travellers, some likening Durham to Jerusalem. Robert Hegge in 1626 in fact claimed that, 'he that hath seene the situation of this Citty, hath seene the Map of Sion, and may save a journey to Jerusalem'.[6] A mere two decades later Dr. Basire, a prebendary of Durham who ignored Hegge's advice and visited the Holy Land, confirmed in detail the similarity between the two cities:

> ... this cittie is an absolute epitome of Jerusalem, nott only for the temple or cathedral, which is a very faire one, standinge uppon the highest hill in the towne, like Mount Sion, but the skirts of the towne resemble Jerusalem, and nott only that, but the country about resembles the country about Jerusalem, beinge, as the scripture saith, a hilly country.[7]

The art of comparison might be seen further with the visit of John Wesley in 1776 when he preached on 'Our Lord's Lamentation over Jerusalem'; certainly the city of Durham at this time was more noted for its high living than for its religious observance. It was presumably this order of priorities that caused a visiting non-conformist minister, James Murray, to observe that 'Durham would be a very fine place, were it not for the swarms of priests.'[8]

Defoe had referred to being in Durham on holiday, a reminder that the observer's frame of mind may be crucial to what is recorded. This, surely, is the explanation of Smollett's description in *The Expedition of Humphry Clinker* in 1771. The final comment would seem to hold the clue to his tone:

> The city in Durham appears like a confused heap of stones and brick, accumulated so as to cover a mountain, round which a river winds its brawling course. The streets are generally

narrow, dark and unpleasant; and many of them almost impassable in consequence of their declivity. The cathedral is a huge, gloomy pile; but the clergy are well lodged. The bishop lives in a princely manner; the golden prebends keep plentiful tables; and, I am told, there is some good sociable company in the place.[9]

A lack of friends in residence is Samuel Johnson's explanation for seeing 'but little' on a visit two years later. His reaction to the 'gloomy pile', however, was more positive than that of Smollett:

The Cathedral has a massiveness and solidity such as I have seen in no other place; It rather awes than pleases, as it strikes with a kind of gigantick dignity.[10]

The second half of the eighteenth century saw the rise of antiquarian-topographers, also a rise in interest in landscape. In County Durham the first major work was by Hutchinson in 1787, the value of which is reflected in the extent of plagiarism among subsequent authors. His survey of the city is notable for the earliest example of the interplay between perspective and landscape experience. The section will repay extensive quotation.

...A few paces from the south road, this English Zion makes a noble appearance. In the centre, the castle and cathedral crown a very lofty eminence, girt by the two streets called the Baileys, enclosed with the remains of the ancient walls, and skirted with hanging gardens and plantations which descend to the river Were, in this point of view exhibiting the figure of a horse-shoe...

Approaching the city from the north, it has the most romantic and uncommon appearance: It seems to be scattered over a multitude of irregular hills ... and we discover various parts of the town, the castle, and churches, through several vallies in one point of view, so that they appear like so many distinct places. The west front of the castle is seen on the summit of a ragged and steep rock, with some parts of the cathedral ... At Castle-Chair, where the view is much confined, the castle and cathedral have a noble appearance: the octagon tower of the former, with the mound on which it is placed, have a grand effect. On the eminence opposite to Shaw Wood, the view just mentioned is enlarged ...

Approaching from the east down the street of St. Giles, we command the second noblest view of the city: In front, the river

Were forms a fine canal through a rich vale, crossed by Elvet bridge, of seven wet arches, and many other land arches; the town crowds the swift risings of the hill, pile upon pile; the castle and cathedral church crowning the summit of the eminence.[11]

The various approaches into the city listed by Hutchinson have been augmented during the nineteenth and twentieth centuries by other particular vantage points from which to view the attractive face of Durham. Perhaps the most commonly experienced view is that from the railway. It was the prospect from just above the railway station that Ruskin observed to be one of the seven wonders of the world. J.B. Priestley's comment on his *English Journey* was that the rail traveller would be 'impressed by the Macbeth-like look of the city'.[12] Although smoke has been largely banished since 1930s, lighting conditions for this north-west prospect may still render his simile apt. The experience of the moving rail traveller is captured in an autobiographical novel by William Conton in 1960:

> ... as the train swung round a curve and over a viaduct, my breath was completely taken away for an instant by the sight of Durham Cathedral ... It seemed to float proudly above the smoky rooftops, gradually turning on its own axis as we described an arc around it, in order, so it seemed, to show itself off to the best advantage.[13]

If Conton's reaction captures the unrepeatable first encounter, it is an informed eye that composes the same scene in James Kirkup's poem, 'Durham seen from the Train':

> The cathedral glides behind the cutting's
> long wave of grass and earth ...
> The traditional escarpment
> crumbles out of sight. The prison
> and the hollow castle fall upon their knees.
> The river turns and disappears into a crust of trees.
> The last houses like a rib lie broken
> on a temporary field invaded by a token pavement.[14]

A terser description, evoking the brevity of the experience, is given by Tony Harrison at the end of his poem, 'Durham', as he leaves on the 6.05 to Plymouth:

> .... As we pull
> out of the station through the dusk and fog,
> there, lighting up, is Durham, dog
> chasing its own cropped tail,
> University, Cathedral, Gaol.[15]

It was the view in the opposite direction, that is, towards the railway from the castle, that Matthew Arnold deemed 'very grand and Edinburghesque', although first prize he gave to the prospect from South Street, with that from Observatory Hill a close second. In a letter referring to his travels in 1861, this visitor from the south could not hide his surprise at the northern city.

> ... when you cross the Wear by the Prebends' Bridge and, ascending through its beautiful skirt of wood, plant yourself on the hill opposite the cathedral, the view of the cathedral and castle together is superb; even Oxford has no view to compare with it ... I was most agreeably disappointed, for I had fancied Durham rising our of a cinder bed. I finished by the observatory, a point on a higher range than the hill just in face of the cathedral, but commanding much the same view in greater perspective.[16]

The view from Prebends' Bridge has been highlighted by many observers. The nineteenth-century American novelist Nathaniel Hawthorne, for instance, recorded in his *English Notebooks* how he:

> paused upon the bridge, and admired and wondered at the beauty and glory of this scene ... it was grand, venerable, and sweet, all at once; I never saw so lovely and magnificent a scene, nor (being content with this) do I care to see a better.[17]

Pevsner, whose task was to evaluate all, considered this prospect the 'most moving one' from which to view 'one of the great experiences of Europe', where the picture of the cathedral rising above the trees appeared 'as it were the vision of a Caspar David Friedrich or Schinkel'. Insertion of a plaque into the bridge containing the well-known lines from 'Harold the Dauntless' referring to the 'grey towers of Durham', has encouraged the spot to become known as 'Scott's view'.

The wooded gorge of the meandering river provides a succession of vantage points for those seeking scenic pleasure. In 1753 the poet Thomas Gray expressed it thus:

> I have one of the most beautiful Vales in England to walk in with prospects that change every ten steps, and open up something new wherever I turn me, all rude and romantic, in short the sweetest Spot to break your neck or drown yourself in that ever was beheld.[18]

One hundred years later the frequent change of prospect beside 'the best of all little rivers' led Hawthorne to believe he and his wife were 'getting into the country', until the reappearance of the cathedral made them realise they 'had made a circuit without our knowing it'. In the present century the surprise of commentators includes the very existence of such rural scenery at the heart of a city.

Another view opened up more recently, which has already taken its place alongside other long-established prospects, is that from the inner relief road, Leazes Road, built in the late 1960s down the Claypath spur. Thomas Sharp had long argued that 'the view

Ye Freshmonne His Adventures at Univ. Coll. Durham.

Ye freshmonne His arrival at ye railway station

and is by no means certain as to where on earth he can be going

but arriving safe at 'The Waterloo' dreams he gets a treble 3rd & is made a Bishop

on the morrow he calleth on the Warden who advises him what to do

after which he goeth to University house to search for rooms

precipitate retreat to ye Castle and taketh rooms in ye keep

dismayed at ye number of steps leading thereto but consoled by ye assurance that he will get used to it in the end

being matriculated he assumeth the cap & gown & under the delusion that they become him

he disporteth himself on the banks to the great amusement of many young ladies

Fig. 7 Some of the Durham sketches by Edward Bradley, c.1850.

from the top of Claypath would really be one of the most magnificent views in Europe',[19] and so it has proved. Lest it be thought that the opinion is biased, since Sharp in fact proposed the road in the 1930s, similar evaluation has come from others, including Ian Nairn, a strong critic of much new development. The revealed, or created, view was 'superb'; the project illustrated how 'a new road can improve a cathedral city.'

While Durham has a setting that has attracted the attention of many commentators and artists, it might be considered somewhat strange that it has never been exploited by any major novelist, although there is no reason per se why painterly beauty should inspire fiction. Indeed, any concentration on its qualities would be at the expense of story. Be that as it may, in the last century there were minor novels by Jane Porter, Annie Raine Ellis and Linnaeus Banks, but the most interesting fiction from this period came from the pen of 'Cuthbert Bede' with various stories of Mr. Verdant Green. The author behind this unoriginal pseudonym was Edward Bradley, a Durham graduate who contributed several sketches to *Punch* before compiling a book of the adventures of freshman Verdant Green at Oxford. The publishers preferred this location, but many of the incidents are drawn from Bradley's experience at University College, Durham. Some of the sketches of this Pickwickian character from which the book originated are shown in Figure 7. The drive from Gilesgate station, the buildings on Palace Green and Prebends' Bridge are easily recognisable in the cartoons.

In the twentieth century novels by Harold Heslop, George Calpin and David Bean have told mining stories, linking the county to the county town through the migration of miners and families to the city for the annual gala. Sid Chaplin, the North-East's major writer, rarely looked to the city in his work. Any suspicion that Durham was the model for the small northern university town of Edgestow in C.S. Lewis' *That Hideous Strength* was refuted by the author. Most recently, Catherine Fox set the first of a trilogy of novels, *Angels and Men*, in Durham, where she captures the city and student life of the 1980s.

Interestingly and ironically, the one novel which has used Durham as an architectural, spiritual and inspirational source is one written by an African, William Conton, quoted earlier. Having received a Western-oriented education in a missionary school, and arriving in England for a university course, the reaction of the hero on first sighting Durham reveals the depth of his acquired western culture.

> The massive towers, the age-mellowed stone whose colour blended so naturally with that of the foliage around it on the banks of the River Wear; above all the mute drama of human faith and achievement played on a stage set by God in the elbow of a river and watched over by the vigilance of eight centuries ... Durham made me realise that, like the work of those Norman builders, my labours must be inspired by considerations other than the purely material, if they were to produce results whose success would have some degree of permanence.[20]

Fig. 8 Prospect of Durham from the south-east, by V. Bok, late 17th century.

Fig. 9 Prospect of Durham from the south-west, by Samuel and Nathaniel Buck.

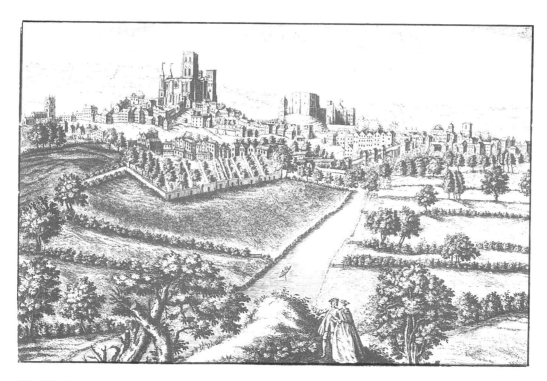

Fig. 10 Prospect of Durham from the east-north-east, by Thomas Forster and James Mynde, 1754.

Fig. 11 Prospect of Durham from the north-west, by Thomas Forster and James Mynde, 1754.

The one work of fiction, then, which enthuses in the manner of commentators – and painters – stems from an observer with a national or international perspective.

The almost theatrical setting of the city has provided a ready topic for a long succession of sketchers and of landscape painters from the time that landscape became an acceptable subject for representation. Not unexpectedly, the vantage points which commentators selected to describe the city were also favoured spots from which to draw or paint. The representative examples illustrated here, chosen from a vast number of possibilities, articulate the different qualities of the city core as its profile is viewed from different angles.

If we disregard a highly inaccurate sketch by King, together with sketches of individual buildings and the representational drawings of the first maps, then the earliest prospect of the city is that by V. Bok (Figure 8). Dateable from its considerable detail to the third quarter of the seventeenth century, the artist's steady hand reveals an emphasis on realism. St. Oswald's church is in the foreground, behind is the prominent city wall running near to the plateau top of the peninsula. Its south-east perspective is replicated by many later drawings from the Mount Joy area.

Around the mid-eighteenth century drawings from three other major perspectives complete an early visual encirclement of the peninsula. The south-west prospect, drawn by Samuel and Nathaniel Buck, is approximately the view from Observatory Hill much painted by subsequent artists (Figure 9). The lowering of the near bank of the meander loop in order to make visible the rise of the southern end of the peninsula should not detract from the essential truthfulness of the recording. The amount and fineness of detail makes it a veritable quarry of information; it also invites a point by point comparison with the description of this particular prospect by Hutchinson, part of which was given earlier in the chapter. To some extent the same is true of the two views by Thomas Forster and James Mynde, although control of perspective is less commanding than that in the effort by the Buck brothers. The view from the north-east, from near Gilesgate, may be considered the early equivalent of the view recently opened up from Leazes Road (Figure 10). In the prospect from the north-west the topography of the Claypath-Gilesgate spine in particular is much exaggerated, while even the major architecture of the peninsula is uncertain (Figure 11). Such licence with realism does not negate its value, however, for, along with other evidence, the trained eye can interpret and interpolate.

The later genre of landscape painting used both the broad vantage points of sketchers as well as closer locations with more confined perspective. The medium of colour also enabled the artist to convey mood as well as topography, so that, at times, today's onlooker of the portrayed scene may feel involved, rather than just a curious spectator of an illustration.

Fig. 12 Durham Cathedral, water-colour by J.M.W. Turner, 1835.

Fig. 13 Durham Castle and Cathedral, water-colour by Thomas Girtin, 1798.

Western, rather then eastern, viewpoints are more common in landscape paintings. Here the elements of river, tree-lined gorge and citadel are more often juxtaposed to spectacular effect. Within the western circuit the most commonly recorded view is the classic arrangement of elements as seen from Prebends' Bridge. Almost all visiting artists have included at least one work from this particular spot, including Edwards, Grimm, Hearne, Girtin, Vaughan, Daniell, Robson, Turner. It is the painting of the last-named that is illustrated here (Figure 12). Although others' works may be more faithful reproductions of the scene, none captures so supremely the sense of place, of Durham. Stylistically a forerunner of impression, the painting gives the cathedral a transcendental quality. The cathedral is turned almost forty-five degrees and in the ethereal colouring of the evening light appears to be rising from the rock on which it is set. The contrived lines of the left-hand trees (cited by Ruskin as among the finest in all painting), distant bridge, weir and Prebends' Bridge parapet all lead the eye to the three towers to complete the spiritual symbolism of the picture.

The second painting is by Turner's early contemporary, Girtin, who generally chose north-east or northern prospects for his paintings of the city. His most forceful work is shown in Figure 13. It was painted in 1798 from a point below Framwellgate Bridge looking upstream into the gorge and to the city on the hill. The valley here has widened, and the neck of the peninsula is colonised by domestic buildings heaped, one upon another, up the slope to the broad summit of the massive citadel. The northern approach was said to be the weak link in the city defences, yet no prospect makes it look more impregnable.

Girtin's painting inspired Cotman to create a similar canvas on his first visit to Durham, but the illustration shown here was executed after his second visit in 1805 (Figure 14). Bringing to bear on Durham an eye trained on gentler East Anglian landscape, he found the city 'delightfully situated' and the cathedral 'magnificent'. The particular perspective here emphasizes the depth of the gorge, the expression highlights the chunky, massive, impregnable qualities of the building. A sombre quality is given to both architecture and foliage.

The final painting illustrated here, with a similar perspective to that adopted by Cotman, celebrates the city's green mantle, at the same time illustrating perhaps that beauty is in the eye of the beholder. Figure 15 is by Mendlessohn after his visit in 1827. A composer of visual music, his painting here displays the music in the river banks' foliage, which surrounds and builds up to the crescendo of the cathedral. That it was the rhythm of the greenery which impressed is shown by the taken-for-granted aspect of some architectural detail. The abbey buildings, for instance, perhaps suggest a southern European location rather than one in northern England.

The observations presented here, whether recorded by pen or brush, has played an active role in the appreciation of the city. Because artists have seen, our vision is enlarged; because they have valued, our pride in place is confirmed. Durham broadcast therefore authenticates, enhances, to a degree, fashions, the city to which we respond.

Fig. 15 Durham, water-colour by Felix Mendelssohn Bartholdy, 1829.

Fig. 14 Durham Cathedral, water-colour by J.S. Cotman, 1805.

3 Durham Appraised: 'One of the Great Architectural Experiences of Europe'

The general architectural merit of Durham is unchallenged. Modern critics who have confirmed its international worth include Sherban Cantacuzino,[1] Alec Clifton-Taylor[2] and William Whitfield[3] although perhaps the most influential survey was that of Nikolaus Pevsner in his Durham volume of the Buildings of England series. Bringing the comparative eye of a mid-European, he declared that:

> Durham is one of the great experiences of Europe to the eyes of those who appreciate architecture, and to the minds of those who understand architecture. The group of Cathedral, Castle, and Monastery on the rock can only be compared to Avignon and Prague.[4]

Moreover, in terms of preservation and greenery he ventured that Durham was superior to its two continental competitors.

The significance and symbolic value of the peninsular group in the evolution of this country were highlighted in the Leader columns of *The Times* in 1944, comment being occasioned by the proposed siting of a power station nearby.

> This is one of the sites on which buildings seem to grow out of their foundations, so that rock and structure form a unity, the Norman builders having been inspired by their opportunity to add loftiness to the strength which is usually the outstanding feature of their work. As a lesson in the significance of the Norman conquest the group is without parallel in England.[5]

While Durham's setting and townscape, rightly, have evoked eulogies, its architecture in more recent times has been subject to detailed, official appraisal. Its buildings have been assessed, structure by structure, and categorised under central government legislation of 1944, whereby the Secretary of State is obliged to maintain a nation-wide list of structures of "special architectural or historic interest." Age, significance and purity are the basis for a three-fold classification of 'listed buildings' into Grade 1 (of exceptional interest), 2* (particular importance) and 2 (special interest). The overwhelming majority of structures in any area are in the last category.

A statistical measure of the architectural endowment of Durham District by this means of appraisal lies less in the number of its listed buildings, than in its proportion of Grade 1 category – nearly three times that of the national average (Table 1).[6] Within the District there is a concentration of listed buildings in the central urban area, which has at its core the old Municipal Borough (Table 2). When plotted, the pattern strongly correlates with early maps of the city, with listed buildings lining its historic entries (Figure 16). This is especially evident in Claypath, leading to Gilesgate and Sunderland, and along Old Elvet, which, with the city's grandest hotel at its head, was the place of assembly from which people arrived or left for London and the south. Road realignment and redevelopment have precluded any similar clustering in the northwest quadrant of historic Framwellgate.

Category Grade	National Average	County Durham	Durham District
1	2.4	3.2	6.7
2*	5.5	5.2	4.8
2	92.1	91.6	88.5

Table 1. Percentage distribution of listed buildings, by grade, 1999.

Category Grade	City Centre	Rest of District
1	47	9
2*	27	13
2	526	207

Table 2. Number of listed buildings in Durham District and City Centre, 1999.

The major historic streets, lined with worthy domestic architecture, lead to the peninsula, where the prominence of the relief is crowned by a concentration of Grade 1 structures, Durham's most precious buildings.[7, 8] Pre-eminent, of course, are the cathedral, with its former abbey buildings, and castle, which together provided the dual focus at the city's foundation and which today are the core of its designation as a World Heritage Site.

The interior of the cathedral is an architectural feast. On entry, the scale and weight of carpentered stone overwhelm, so that it is some time before the eye turns to discern the structural details which enabled the Norman innovators to complete the building by cladding the roof, seventy feet above, in stone. The prominent feature of pairs of massive alternate rounded and clustered pillars marching the length of the nave was not repeated when extensions were added soon after completion of William of St. Calais' original design. At the west end, the Galilee Chapel illustrates that lightness of touch was also within the repertoire of Romanesque masons. At the east end, the Chapel of Nine Altars achieves towering height by a combination of lower floor level, long lancet windows and fluted pillars composed of a series of alternating columns of Frosterley marble and sandstone. As an enlarged replacement of the original apsidal east end, it was designed to provide a more generous space for pilgrims attracted to the once-sumptuous shine of St Cuthbert.

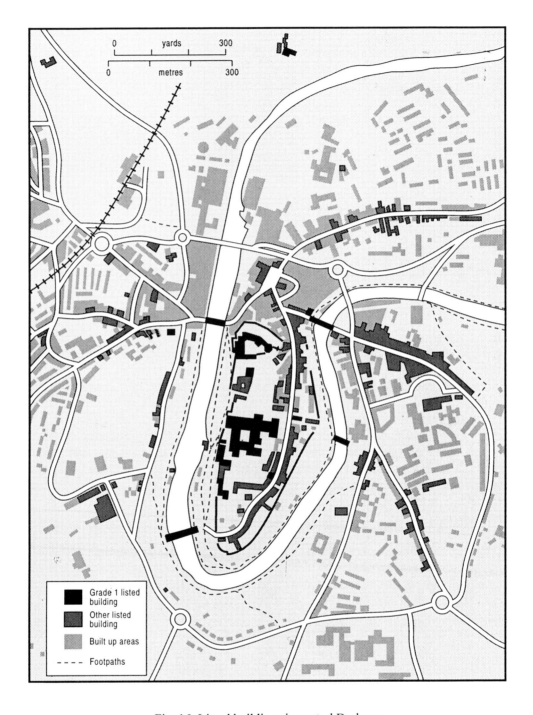

Fig. 16 Listed buildings in central Durham.

28

Other architectural highlights within the cathedral include the medieval wall paintings in the Galilee Chapel; the 14th century Neville Screen behind the high altar, where the frozen music of its Perpendicular finery in Caen stone is composition enough, without reflecting on some hundred statues lost at the Dissolution; the 17th century sculptural woodwork of Bishop Cosin, flanking the chancel and acknowledging the Neville Screen to which it leads; also Cosin's exuberant font canopy, over forty foot high; lastly, the north door, with its sanctuary knocker seen on entry, and the two original 13th century south doors with their original ironwork leading from the cathedral to cloister and former Benedictine monastery (See Figure 45).

The whole of the west range of the former monastery is occupied by the Monks' Dormitory (c.1400), notable for its original forty-foot baulk oak timber roof. Running the length of the 200 foot dormitory, it resembles the upturned hull of some mighty galleon. The layout of the monks' cubicles can be deduced from the arrangement of the tall, two-light Perpendicular windows. Beyond the south range is the Prior's Kitchen. Built between 1366 – 74 by John Lewyn, the lobed stone arches of this octagonal building form a complex patterned vault unlike anything elsewhere in England. Angled lighting as part of its recent conversion to a bookshop has articulated the engineering feat with a clarity denied surely even to the original architect. Nearby, in its walled garden, is the Deanery, formerly the Prior's Lodging. Its 13th century base with a subsequent patchwork is blended harmoniously with Georgian restyling; it has been called 'Barchester' at its best. Across the green, two of the prebendal or canons' houses, outwardly Georgian but concealing portions of the medieval monastery, are also Grade 1, as are further units of the west, or top, end of this peaceful architectural space known as The College.

The castle, originally the episcopal palace, complements the cathedral, which it actually predates. Its north wing contains the earliest Norman structure in Durham: the crypt chapel, dated 1071. Its column arrangement of a short nave and two side aisles carrying a grid of groin vaults, plus its herring-bone flagstones, is time preserved. The spatial compression of the womb-like structure also constitutes memorable acoustic architecture. Above the chapel was the original great hall of Bishop Hugh of Le Puiset, now divided on two floors, although the grand ceremonial entrance remains, protected since the 16th century by the Tunstall Gallery. On the second floor the Norman Gallery announces itself, with deep, colonnaded wall seats beneath chevron arches. (The evident structural 'leaning' is the consequence of the palace resting on sand and gravel, and not bedrock. The tilt was stabilised – and the whole castle saved – by an international rescue effort in the 1930s).

The north range of the castle is joined to that of the west by the Black Staircase, commissioned by Bishop Cosin. One of the most famous in England, its ornately-carved balustrade panels rise through four floors, being cantilevered into the walls and originally free-standing. The west wing contains the present great hall, one of the finest in the country, constructed above the Norman undercroft by Bishop Bek at the turn of the 14th century, and enlarged by Bishop Hatfield, only to be truncated by Bishop Fox at the end of the 15th century in order to insert kitchens, which are themselves no less impressive.

The ovens are beneath magnificent stone arches, surrounded by some of the oldest brickwork in the north of England.

Two other prominent structures, each separately listed, are the irregular octagonal keep rebuilt by Salvin (1840), and the gatehouse, heavily restored by Wyatt (1800), although the older dark oak door with standard ironwork does its best to suggest greater antiquity for the whole piece. The Grade 1 sequence is completed just beyond the gatehouse by the former Exchequer, Chancery and Palatinate Court of Bishop Neville (1457). A thrusting bull's head, the bishop's crest, denotes the present modest building.

On the peninsula's North Bailey, in the shadow of the east end of the cathedral, stands the church of St. Mary-le-Bow. Originally one of two medieval garrison churches within the castle walls, and now a Heritage Centre, its Grade 1 listing stems primarily from the quality of its late 17th and early 18th century woodwork in the Cosin tradition. It was installed following the rebuilding of the church, 1671-85. The original church was partially destroyed in 1635 in the collapse of part of the adjoining medieval gate ('bow') across the Bailey. The present west front with its doorway and niche above and two lights remain from the earlier church.

The rim of the peninsula is delineated by the extensive listed sections of its medieval defensive wall (Figure 16). On the east side preserved sections are in most gardens of properties lining the Baileys, with the best being at the extreme southern limit before it meets the southern postern gate, Watergate. (Repositioned in the late 18th century, its plain semi-circular arch has remnants of the cathedral's original rose-window tracery curiously perched above it). On the west side, most impressive is the central section between the Dark Entry (to the monastery) and Windy Gap (site of a former postern, now a vennel, to Palace Green). With the aid of buttresses, it supports former monastic buildings and the Galilee Chapel in their precarious sites above the river. A notable feature in the northern defences is a two-storey, 14th century bastion. (This is visible through the grill of a door at the top right-hand side of Saddler Street.)

The listed historic bridges giving access to the peninsula further emphasise the architectural importance of the core. The neck of the peninsula is joined by the two Norman bridges: Bishop Flambard's Framwellgate Bridge, with its two wide eliptical arches, in the shadow of the castle, and Bishop Le Puiset's Elvet Bridge, with its two wide eliptical arches, in the shadow of the castle, and Bishop Le Puiset's Elvet Bridge, with its multiple arches on a steep ascent to the city. Just beyond the southern end of the river loop is Prebends' Bridge, designed by George Nicholson, the Cathedral Architect, in 1778. Although the eye is normally directed *from* the bridge, its three high, semi-circular arches and balustrading can be well appreciated from the banks' footpaths, where the sedate flow of water often allows the observer to see double. A fourth crossing has recently achieved Grade 1 listing, namely Kingsgate Bridge. A sculpture in reinforced concrete by Ove Arup (1963), its taut high-level footbridge echoes the high ribbed vault of Bishop William of St. Calais. (Postwar structures did not become eligible for listing until 1987, when it was decided that thirty years must elapse after construction before consideration could be given. Kingsgate Bridge was listed in 1996; only one other modern bridge in the country has similar status.)

A review of Grade 1 buildings is completed by four structures distributed in an arc around the northern end of the peninsula. Two of the three medieval churches with substantial extant evidence of Norman beginnings are listed – St. Margaret's and St. Giles'. (It is ironic that the one omitted is St. Oswald's, for dedication, as well as written and archaeological evidence, suggest it is the oldest ecclesiastical site in the city. Its lower listing is presumably attributable to mining subsidence, which necessitated rebuilding of the east end amid extensive 19th century restoration. On the other hand, 'historic interest' was enhanced through having as incumbent, John Bacchus Dykes, the most prolific hymn-writer of the Victorian era).

St. Giles', on an elevated site at Gilesgate, was founded as a chapel of Bishop Flambard's hospital at Kepier in the Wear Valley below. It subsequently became the church for its borough and planned settlement, which was created by Norman clearance of the earliest peninsular dwellings. At Kepier today, the architectural highlights are an impressive vaulted hospital gatehouse, rebuilt in 1341 after being fired by the Scots, and parts of a 16th century mansion among adjoining farm buildings. On the opposite bank, nearer the city, is a more complete, if complex, composition of a manor house, Crook Hall. Its 14th century stone hall, with minstrels' gallery, is attached to a 17th century gabled extension, which in turn is attached to a tall three-storey Georgian townhouse, all enclosed by pleasant walled gardens. Of all listed structures, it constitutes the city's most precious secular building.

Structure	Year Completed	Architect	Awarding Body
Awards:			
Kingsgate Bridge	1963	Ove Arup	CT, CS
University Library	1966	George Pace	CT
Dunelm House	1967	Michael Powers	CT
Trevelyan College	1967	J.Eastwick-Field	CT
Collingwood College	1973	Richard Sheperd	RIBA
New Elvet Bridge	1975	John R Tully	CS
Millburngate 1	1976	Building Design Partnership	CT; EN
Centre Floorscaping	1978	Anthony RN Scott	CT
Commendations:			
Owengate Houses	1965	David Roberts, Geoffrey Clarke	CT
Van Mildert College	1968	Philip Middleton	CT
Jevons House, Hatfield College	1968	Bernard Taylor	CT
University Psychology Building	1969	William Whitfield	CT
Abbey House	1974	David Roberts, Geoffrey Clarke	EA
Leazes Bowl Carpark	1975	William Whitfield	RIBA
Extension, St. Aidan's College	1981	Faulkner Brown	CT
Fellows Gdn, University College	1994	Dennis Jones	CT

Table 3. Architectural awards and commendations.' (EA – European Architectural Heritage Year; EN - Europa Nostra; CS – Concrete Society; CT – Civic Trust; RIBA -- Royal Institute of British Architects).

In view of the severely restricted application of listing appraisal to postwar buildings, the best substitute indication of architectural quality among modern constructions is in recognition by international and national bodies, most notably the Civic Trust and the Royal Institute of British Architects. By this criterion the architectural stock of the city has been enriched by eight structures which have received awards, while another eight have received commendation (Table 3). The 1960s and 70s appear as the most fruitful decades, while the university can be seen as the major patron. Three structures are especially significant.

First, and most extensive, is the floorscaping of the central streets between Framwellgate and Elvet Bridges, including the Market Place (1975-78). Designed by Anthony Scott, the City Planning Officer, the 10,000 square metres of paving has played a key role in unifying the central area. Second-hand York paving flags, with York setts enclosing central 'wheelers', have retained the street as a linear feature, united the flanking properties and evoked a historical context.

Second, Millburngate Centre (1) achieved the most prestigious award, a Europa Nostra Award, in 1976, acclaim widely disseminated through its depiction on a U.K. postage stamp in a series commemorating urban renewal (Figure 17). The break-up of the brick mass, the irregular roof line, riverside flats echoing the bow-windowed premises replaced, and the tying into the bridgehead, all show respect for quality of place. Building Design Partnership managed to incorporate some 68,000 square feet of retailing as well as a medium-sized car park within the structure.

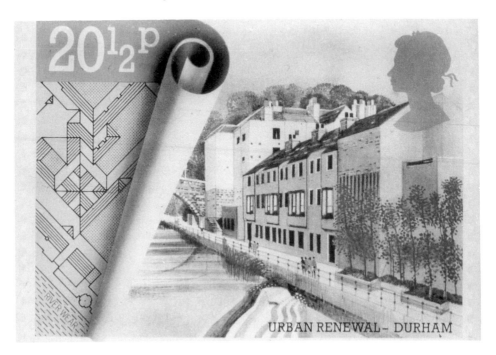

Fig. 17 Millburngate Centre 1, depicted on U.K. postage stamp, 1984.

The third structure is Kingsgate Bridge, uniquely listed, as mentioned above. In sculptural terms it forms a single composition with Dunelm House, designed by Michael Powers (1965). The latter building is strikingly innovative, the only example of Brutalist architecture in the city, as it stands guard at the entry to the gorge section of the river (See Figure 25).

Hardly less significant is the University Library extension by George Pace (1966). Here, the architect succeeded in the most daunting of tasks of slotting a large contemporary construction between cathedral and castle. In fact the stone-clad building neither fronts onto, nor can be seen from, Palace Green, but the dimensions of the several-storeyed building can be appreciated from Broken Walls or South Street.

Set among parkland, immediately south of the river loop, are six university colleges: two received awards, a third, a commendation. Trevelyan College (H. Stillman and J. Eastwick-Field, 1967) is an essay in hexagonal geometry, perhaps drawing its inspiration from the keep of the castle. In springtime the dark brick composition is set in a sea of daffodils. Landscaping, however, is above all a feature of Collingwood College (Sir Richard Sheperd, 1973), where the brick massing and mature trees interlock in one composition; it is as if what we call 'landscaping' for the new built form was conceived and planted half-a-century before. Of the other colleges, Van Mildert (Philip Middleton, 1966), with its waterscape and cloistered walk of exceptional quality, received an architectural commendation, but, rather surprisingly, St. Aidan's (Sir Basil Spence, 1965) did not. Set on a knoll giving a wonderful panorama of the city, yet curiously unobtrusive as a skyline feature, the building is a monumental essay of solids and voids incorporating features characteristic of the architect's repertoire.

The architectural highlights of an historic city, by definition, derive from its venerable buildings. In Durham so powerful was the initial Romanesque statement that for centuries it overshadowed any small subsequent growth. In architectural terms, after modest pre-industrial elegance, a relatively weak industrial response has slowly yielded to increasing post-industrial pressure which could threaten the traditional face of the city. In future, therefore, independent appraisal *before* construction must assume greater importance in order, to ensure that tradition continues to be re-invented in each generation. Such a strategy is the best insurance against possible dilution of an architectural assemblage considered to constitute one of the great experiences of Europe.

4   Durham Experienced: Sensing and Making Sense of the City'

There is no single image of Durham. Differences in first- and second-hand knowledge, or between knowledge and experience, ensure that we each hold a particular, maybe idiosyncratic, view of the city. Durham, for instance, is likely to be viewed differently by a resident, property developer, traffic engineer, tourist, student, inmate of Durham gaol, or whatever. Age, gender and class will incur their own broad variations. The two worlds of experience summarised here are those of insider and outsider, the source being a questionnaire with statistically-respectable samples of residents and tourists.[1]

Sensing

One indication of the relative importance of the different senses is given in Table 4. The overwhelming importance of the visual contribution is evident, even though the request was to cite examples from different senses. A striking feature, however, is the fact that the tourist, and not resident, image apparently puts relatively less emphasis on the visual input and more on feelings. The greater relative emphasis on feelings may be a function of the group's more homogeneous current state. Given an initial encounter, a city deliberately chosen and presumably anticipated, and a visit undertaken for pleasure and not business or routine, one can hypothesise a particular frame of mind with a heightened perception. Moreover, this recently acquired image is tapped while still fresh, before sharpness of detail and evaluation are dulled by time and separation. Residents differ in this respect in that, although no physical severance from the city is involved, yet the very familiarity can breed neglect in that many items may glide imperceptibly into a passive state of acceptance, no longer evoking conscious arousal and evaluation. Detail may be lost, and the temporary neglected, where there is no longer the need or willingness to sustain the initial interest. These several features can be illustrated from a list of the most frequently mentioned items for each of the senses (Table 5).

Respondent Group	Number of Subjects	Mean No of Entries	Percentage Distribution by Category			
			Sights	Sounds	Smells	Feelings
Tourists	59	8.7	61	15	11	13
Residents	94	9.9	70	14	8	8

Table 4. Characteristic Image: Percentage Distribution by Sense Modality Categories

In the tourists' image building reconstruction is ranked as the fourth leading characteristic sight, following the expected trio of cathedral, castle and river, which are the leading items in the visual image of both groups. In complete contrast, the residents' image contains but one mention of change. [Change was rife in the central area at the time of survey – with the Millburngate Shopping Centre, Leazes Bowl Carpark and New Elvet Bridge under construction]. Only tourists rank narrow streets as characteristic sights or include the Market Place police box within the leading sights. Again, tourists, who as a group not only see but actually visit the cathedral, alone include details of the cathedral interior as a characteristic sight of the city, it being the ninth-ranking item.

Turning to the sonic environment, outsiders rank noise of traffic above the sound of bells, whereas residents reverse the order. A connection between length of acquaintance and receptability may be evoked again here, in that residents may incline to list what ought to be characteristic rather than undertake a more personal recall. The wording of one entry of a resident living near the centre admitted such as action: 'Of course I realise the cathedral bells ring, but I cannot honestly say I notice them'.

Outsiders rank the sound of cathedral music or service, while residents give it not a single mention. Their equivalent entry perhaps is the brass bands of the annual miners' gala day. Accents rank the third most notable element for the tourists but were absent for residents. In its place residents rank trains, a noise unrecorded by the largely motor-borne tourist.

	TOURISTS		RESIDENTS	
Sights	Cathedral	90	Cathedral	69
	River	49	Castle	61
	Castle	46	River	57
	Reconstruction	19	Market Place	36
	Market Place	17	River Banks	35
	Narrow Streets	17		
	Trees	17		
Sounds	Traffic	31	Bells	38
	Bells	24	Traffic	30
	Accents	15	Trains	19
	Lack of Sound	12	Gala Bands	10
	Cathedral Service	10	Rowers	7
Smells	Traffic Fumes	19	Traffic Fumes	16
	River	12	Fish and Chips	12
	Riverside Flowers	7	Stall Market	11
	Trees, Undergrowth	7	River	10
	Gas	5	Fresh Air	5
Feelings	Peacefulness	12	Peacefulness	12
	Frustration	12	Contentment	9
	Annoyance	12	Change	9
	History	8	Friendliness	5
	Awe	7	History	4
	Welcome	7	Learning	4

Table 5: Characteristic Image: Most frequently mentioned Items, by Sense Modality (Percentage of Respondents Recording)

One subtle difference in the sonic environment associated with the river is that whereas residents, being conscious of the shouts of cox and coach for much of the university year, list rowers, visitors record the less specific entry of boating, referring mostly to the hire of pleasure boats. The tourist, with a shorter stay, is, in fact, struck by the absence of sound, resulting presumably from a greater proportion of time spent in the cathedral precincts and river banks by Prebends' Bridge.

The more circumscribed movement of outsiders is reflected in the leading entries of the smelled environment. The river and its wooded banks are an attraction for the tourist, whereas the resident more readily recalls those general elements of the city encountered in everyday living. Thus, fish and chips is considered the second most characteristic smell of the city. For both insiders and outsiders, however, traffic fumes is the most characteristic feature. [The removal of traffic from the central shopping streets was not possible until the later completion of New Elvet Bridge]. The slow movement of a heavy column of traffic through the narrow streets of the centre thus provides the characteristic sound and smell of Durham – not the most propitious of images by which to recall a cathedral city.

Peacefulness is considered the leading feeling engendered by the city. For tourists, however, this feeling and associated ones of history, learning, awe, etc., are balanced by those of annoyance and/or frustration. The ceaseless battle with traffic, inadequate sign-posting and paucity of eating places and public toilets are the most frequent cause of adverse feelings during the tourists' characteristically brief sojourn. [Happily, the causes of these negative comments have since been considerably ameliorated]. The residents, putting less premium on time and employing a less critical comparative inquisitiveness, may well have grown to overlook such conditions and recall instead the more positive features.

Making Sense

The experience of Durham as a coherent entity may be tapped through a mental mapping exercise, the assumption being that we make sense of the different elements and parts of the city by mentally knitting them together to form a spatial image. Despite questions of validity of an exercise based on introspection and cartographic ability, the drawn maps, together with accompanying annotation and comments, provide interesting material from which to detect certain characteristics of the city as it is perceived to be – the city of the mind. Figure 18 gives examples of some common cartographic expressions.

Durham is foremost a city of surprise and confusion. These are qualities which adhere to any town on an initial encounter and which recede in importance with increasing acquaintance as the several parts are identified and cohere to an overall pattern. The nature of these qualities, therefore, is more likely to be tapped from the heightened perception of outsiders, although residents who have 'grown used' to the same scenes, when challenged in an exercise such as the present, may still yield evidence

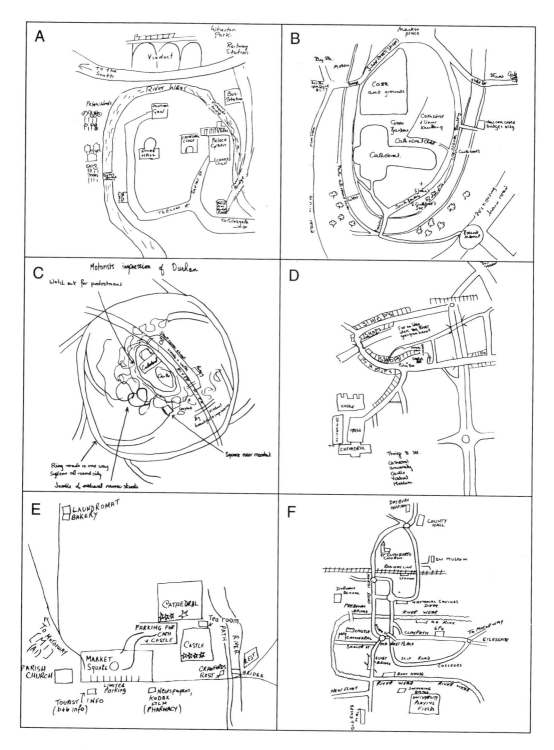

Fig. 18 Examples of mental maps of Durham drawn by tourists and residents.

to show that their knowledge acceptance is idiosyncratic and does not necessarily correspond to that of the objective world.

The primary reason for Durham being an apparently confusing city is that its structure violates what psychologists term the laws of good figure. Inference of expected sequence or symmetry from the normal props to navigation and mental structuring are of little value in Durham. The river is perhaps the prime culprit here. On its meandering course through the city it has reduced the neck of the peninsula to a mere 200 metres, although at street level this is not apparent. A looping gorge hides or interrupts any continuous view, while two weirs conceal the direction of flow for much of its course. There is no obvious left and right bank. Rather, the river keeps reappearing; in the words of one new resident, 'it seems to be always around you'. In short, the river provides no instantly legible frame of reference.

The result may be confusion as to the size and content of the peninsula. For two visitors the loop of the river enclosed not only the cathedral, but Old Shire Hall and the gaol as well (Figure 18a). The position of the river in the Old Elvet area was also a problem to several outsiders, while there was a tendency to exaggerate the size of the cathedral (18b) and to assume a central or end position on the peninsula for the building.

Legibility was not necessarily improved in the short-term experience by the construction of Leazes Road as a relief to the Claypath entry, for the two roads cross twice, like the intersecting arcs of two circles, at Gilesgate roundabout and at the Claypath underpass. In the central core the busy, winding and narrow streets, converging on the Market place with its unique system of traffic control, presented a formidable challenge to the tourist who arrived by car. In the words of one of them:

> Once you're in you're on your own. Street signs are there if you
> can find them. You'll probably end going round in circles
> though.

Another referred to 'the maze of streets threading in and out and up and down'. The stiffness of the challenge which Durham presents is epitomised in the terse addendum to the map of a touring German – 'only city I got lost in twice'.

The clue to navigation, and to the structure of the city, was spotted by one tourist who, after a four-hour visit, deduced

> The city is at first very confusing until you realise you can walk
> and drive around a large circle.

The map, shown in Figure 18c and headed 'Motorist's Impression of Durham', clearly shows the circular ring road of which planners have talked for decades. In such an idealised map it is interesting to speculate that it would have been too much of a good thing to have expected a similar course for the river, which here has a straight course and leaves by flowing beneath the railway viaduct.

A more common perception among motorists, particularly those entering or leaving from the north-east, was the exaggerated importance given to Leazes Road. Several referred to the 'motorway' or 'motorway bypass'. Figure 18d is a classic example of this type. The whole map evolves from the central spine of a large divided carriageway of a road which in reality is three lanes. In contrast, tourists entering and returning by the southern route may relegate in importance, or even omit, Leazes Road from the map. The value of the Market Place as an anchor to some tourists finds expression in its exaggerated importance in the maps. Figure 18e, drawn by an American, even depicts the car-parking spaces as well as key shops and a star-rating for the tourist highspots.

Apart from the knowledge that one can circumnavigate the peninsula, half a dozen respondents – none of them tourists – recommended that the positions of the cathedral and castle be taken as a guide to orientation. Given the various points in the city, long used by artists and photographers, it is perhaps surprising that more reference was not made to this potential. The cathedral serves not only as a beacon from many parts, but as one where silhouette changes as perspective varies. Anyone familiar with Durham will appreciate the imagery of the American tourist who, noting this phenomenon, remarked that from one part of the city the cathedral looked like the QE2 while from another angle like Apollo 13 on its launching pad.

Durham, however, is a city of ups and downs, a description used by several respondents. In consequence, the traveller is continually changing both direction and angle, such that intervisibility is frequently restricted. Together with the enclosed, domestic scale of the architecture, it means that the cathedral is concealed from view on the traditional route from the Market Place until the very last minute as the pilgrim ascends Owengate and reaches Palace Green. Being a classic example of what Sharp termed an approach with a delayed but unbarred climax,[2] means that the cathedral cannot at the same time provide an uninterrupted navigational beacon.

Surprise is an integral quality of the Durham townscape, stemming from a variety of building and vista. For outsiders, surprise begins at the very entry of the city, whether the arrival be by train or car. The indelible imprint from the railway of the sudden appearance of the peninsular group rising above the domestic roofscape has remained the symbolic image of several long-term residents. The preservation of park-like landscape to the south, the construction of a bypass for the old A1 in the west and a slip road from the motorway in the north-east mean that entries to the city are not preceded by a gradual build-up of suburbia. One tourist marked on the map the point where the city would be sighted, with a brief annotation, 'be prepared for a shock.' In the words of another tourist,

> As you approach Durham (from the north) you seem suddenly to
> be in the city. It is a rapid transition from pleasant countryside

to the streets of the city with no (or little) sprawling suburbia.
All of a sudden you see the sight of the cathedral and castle on
the hill and suddenly you are in the mish-mash of the crowded
narrow streets of the town centre.

It is the rapidity of the transition just described that turns the quality of surprise – temporarily at least – into one of confusion for the newcomer. Little wonder, moreover, that he or she may register that the city is 'not far from any part of the countryside; in fact it is a countryside town', or that it 'appears to have no very poor or slummy areas.'

Increased acquaintance brings with it a more balanced appreciation. Numerous references by residents to 'surprising', 'unexpected', 'intriguing', 'inexhaustible' are a tribute to the depth and variety of interest of a city which has as its climax a highly imageable building where visual and social prominence coincide. At the same time however, it is interesting to note that people acquainted with the city make sense of the overall structural form by increasing its goodness or symmetry (18f). As a city of the mind, therefore, Durham is a blend of the ideal and idealised. Expressed in more prosaic terms, although Durham is a highly imageable city, it is not one which is immediately legible or coherent.

5   Durham Captured: A Photographic Essay

A camera has been called an image-freezing machine, able to capture the world, recording reality as it is. Such a statement, however, suggests a mastery which the camera does not possess. The camera's eye is subject to a myriad of human decisions – time and lighting, composition, angle, lens, speed, focusing, and so on. As a result, a photograph may be a rendering as much as a recording, with the power to suggest, evoke or encapsulate a subject no less than does a painting. In this photo-essay, therefore, the illustrations are the text, in which various qualities – or experiences – of Durham or Durhamness are presented for contemplation.

*

A view outwards *from* the cathedral tower, reversing the normal gaze, confirms the ground-level experience of greenness (Figure 19). Although height has smoothed relief, the encircling defile of the river gorge is still discernible. In the more conventional direction, juxtaposition of river, medieval bridge and high peninsula crowned by the cathedral is a recurring composition (Figure 20). One unexpected variation is where the cathedral towers provide the focal point for the workaday secular foreground of city centre allotments (Figure 21).

Within the town, a closed vista and varied floorscape prevail, from main shopping streets to the humble lane leading to the stonemasons' yard in The College (Figures 22,23). There is no street called Straight in Durham: all take their cue from the river and curve tantalisingly, the bend in their course forming a question mark which encourages the imagination to roam and invites further exploration. Something always remains to be seen or understood. Thus do mystery and disclosure combine.

There is no mystery in the boldness, as bright as the sunshine, reflected in the façade of South Street on the lip of the gorge opposite the peninsula's theatre of the sublime (Figure 24).   Acceptable as architecture, the units together constitute memorable townscape. Bold also is the 1960s composition of Dunelm House by Michael Powers and Ove Arup's Kingsgate Bridge (Figure 25). Shuttered or reinforced concrete unites the brutalist bulk of the former with the slim elegance of the river crossing.

Early cobbles and Westmorland slate, with later setts, second-hand York stone and unifying central wheelers of the 1970s floorscaping scheme, together provide interest underfoot in central streets. Historical interest is added for those who spot the hexagon of granite setts in the market Place, for it marks the site of the pant, source of the city's only public water supply for two centuries and sole architectural marker in the square until joined by the equestrian statue in the mid-19th century (Figure 26). A different history was recorded in the floorscaping scheme by inclusion among the second-hand York stone of part of a former tombstone, its inscription confirming for this stone at least a previous

Fig. 19 View to south-west from Cathedral tower.

Fig. 20 Elvet Bridge and peninsula.

Fig. 21 St. Margaret's allotments.

Fig. 22 South Bailey.   Fig. 23 Way to masons' yard, The College.

use (Figure 27). Dotted about the pavements are the initials 'M.H.' which could be mistaken as the work of a modern stonemason; they, in fact, indicate public utilities beneath (Figure 28). Actually, symbols, rather then letters, were the signatures of medieval craftsmen who cut the stone for cathedral and castle (Figure 29).

The stone out of which Durham was constructed to such monumental effect, at close quarters can exhibit not only inherent beauty but also vulnerability. Differences in iron content, cross-bedding and in quarry cutting of the Lower Carboniferous Sandstone, mean that its carving may release an additional art form in the colourful swirl of grains (Figure 30). Exposed to the outside elements, the cut stone may weather into filigreed sculpture (Figure 31).

Sooner or later, whether resident or visitor, one comes eye-to-eye with the feline face on the cathedral north door (Figure 32) Universally, if misleadingly, known as the Knocker, it is today an icon of curiosity and photo stop. In the past, the interest would have been in deadly earnest; grasping the ring could literally have been a matter of life and death to the medieval fugitive seeking sanctuary.

What is the city but the people? Daily, weekly, seasonal rhythms constitute the city

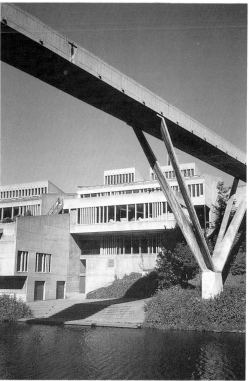

Fig. 24 South Street.   Fig. 25 Dunelm House and Kingsgate Bridge.

heartbeat.   Every Friday and Saturday the open market provides both a sonic and olfactory feast amid the temporary visual street theatre (Figure 33). While the 1990s may have seen the closure of the county's last pit, the contribution of coal mining to its heritage dictates that the annual miners' gala continues. Although broadened in scope, banners, bands, speeches and cathedral service still mark the second Saturday in July (Figure 34). A little earlier in the summer, Palace Green is ablaze with the university graduation days, while the river hosts a weekend of racing during the country's oldest regatta.

Lighting and weather and season affect mood of both person and place. Serenity is induced by the play of light and shadow articulating the Gothic tracery of the cathedral cloister in the late summer afternoon sun with a clarity matched by the stillness of the place (Figure 35). At night, the angled illumination of the varied lighting puts on a display which differs markedly from that of the fuller day-time vision of bridge and peninsula, when the eye is less directed (Figure 36).

The river gorge, which brings the peninsula into being, and which both completes and complements the scene visually, is a world in its own right. The Wear itself is ever

Fig. 26 Site of Pant in Market Place.

Fig. 27 Gravestone incorporated in floorscape.

Fig. 28 Public utility marker.

Fig. 29 Cathedral stonemason's mark.

changing. Flow, amount and provenance of suspended material, degree of surface ruffling or reflection, and colour of Banks and sky together compose a ceaseless and ceaselessly changing symphony. The passage of seasons, recorded from the same vantage point, suggest it is not only the philosopher who is unable to step into the same river twice (Figures 37-40). Weather, no less than seasonal change, can kindle a particular sense of place. The last skeins of a lingering mist is an appropriate context for a sudden glimpse of Wilbourn's Kathedra sculpture on the opposite bank, and in sympathy with the artful landscaping of the 18th century picturesque (Figure 41). Mist is turned into mystery when looking into a low winter sun with dampness in the air in the vicinity of Prebends' Bridge (Figure 42). Another day, and clarity and stillness of air paint a perfectly-reflected image of the same bridge (Figure 43). Again, a breath of wind and the shimmering impermanence of light converts it to an impressionistic rendering (Figure 44). By such means does beauty in the natural world encourage one to stand and stare, at the same time complementing the response to the awe-inspiring beauty within the temple on the hill which human hands have made.

Fig. 30 Swirl of sandstone grains, cathedral.

Fig. 32 Cathedral Knocker.

Fig. 31 Eroded sandstone.

Fig. 33 Market Place, activity.

Fig. 34 Miners' Gala parade.

Fig. 35 Light and shadow in Cathedral cloister.

Fig. 36 Night illumination by Framwellgate Bridge.

49

Fig. 37 Count's Corner, spring-time.

Fig. 38 Count's Corner, summer.

Fig. 39 Count's Corner, autumn.

Fig. 40 Count's Corner, winter.

Fig. 41 Kathedra sculpture on River Banks.

Fig. 42 Prebends' Bridge, winter mist.

Fig. 43 Prebends' Bridge, summer stillness.

Fig. 44 Impressionist reflection of Prebends' Bridge.

6   Durham Cathedral: 'The Best Building in the World'

All cathedrals are worthy of attention, respect and awe, for they are monuments housing more than one layer of meaning. Nowhere is this more evident than at Durham, where the ecclesiastical icon is also an architectural innovation, an aesthetic high and a cultural benchmark. Its international significance was acknowledged by UNESCO in 1986 when it was designated a World Heritage Site. Two years earlier the cathedral had received the appellation of 'the best building in the world.' The occasion was the 150th anniversary of the Royal Institute of British Architects, when the *Illustrated London News* commissioned some fifty experts to assess the world's leading man-made constructions.[1] Durham Cathedral was a convincing winner, ahead even of the Taj Mahal and Parthenon, which were in second and third places, respectively. While the result may have been of little surprise to locals, in a wider context any charge of ethnocentrism can be tempered by the comparable rating awarded by American commentator Bill Bryson – 'best cathedral on planet Earth'[2] – and by knowledge that, long before recent acclamations, a host of scholars and critics have ranked the cathedral in international terms. By the highest standard, then, the cathedral on the rock of Durham peninsula is a noteworthy building, an icon worthy of our contemplation.

Architecture

Durham Cathedral is where the structural thrust problem in major buildings was resolved, where the buttress, rib-vault and pointed arch of the Gothic were first demonstrated, albeit in a Romanesque, or Norman, construction. The achievement, according to Pevsner in his *Outline of European Architecture*, represented 'the ultimate fulfilment of that tendency towards articulation which had driven Romanesque architects forward for over a hundred years.'[3] The architectural, or engineering, achievement was an international one, with the skill and imagination of William of St. Calais and his Norman builders bringing to fruition the accumulated wisdom from contacts further afield in southern Europe – with ecclesiastical buildings in Lombardy and with Islamic work in southern Spain. But it was at Durham that the vision was realised.

The speed of construction was remarkable, with the whole building being completed within forty years of laying the foundation stone in 1093 (Figure 45). Building material was near to hand, initially cut stone from the dismantling of the recently erected Saxon cathedral, and then from quarries on the sides of the river gorge and from just beyond the west bank. The cathedral was thus constructed of the same rock, the Low Main Post, or 'Cathedral', Sandstone, on which it stands. Uniformity of material, allied to speed of erection – and restraint in subsequent restorations – has produced a building of remarkable purity. Since it is also 'by far and away the best proportioned of all Norman cathedrals,'[4] it constitutes the most perfect example of late Romanesque (Figure 46). In context it represents the supreme architectural creation of a period when this country was at the forefront of European art in general.[5] As a consequence, the cathedral of Durham is a building by which others are judged and a place of pilgrimage for any serious student of architecture.

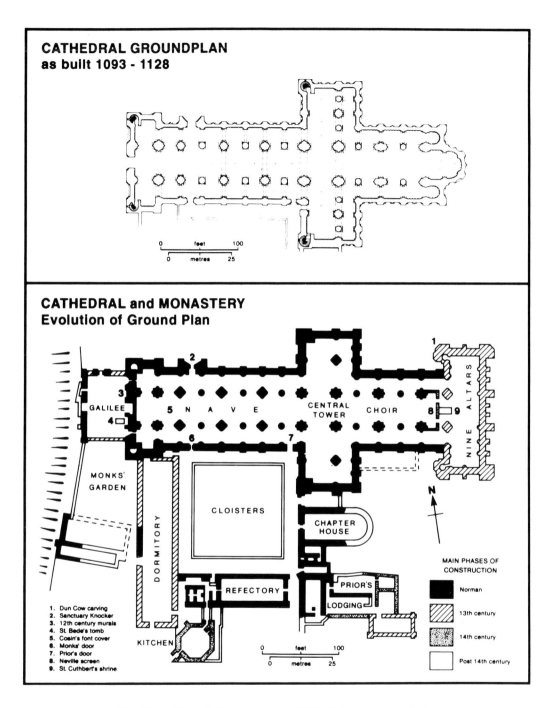

**CATHEDRAL GROUNDPLAN
as built 1093 - 1128**

**CATHEDRAL and MONASTERY
Evolution of Ground Plan**

GALILEE

CENTRAL
TOWER

CHOIR

NINE ALTARS

5   N A V E

MONKS'
GARDEN

DORMITORY

CLOISTERS

CHAPTER
HOUSE

REFECTORY

PRIOR'S
LODGING

KITCHEN

1. Dun Cow carving
2. Sanctuary Knocker
3. 12th century murals
4. St. Bede's tomb
5. Cosin's font cover
6. Monks' door
7. Prior's door
8. Neville screen
9. St. Cuthbert's shrine

MAIN PHASES OF
CONSTRUCTION

Norman

13th century

14th century

Post 14th century

Fig. 45(a) Cathedral ground plan, (b) Evolution of ground plan.

55

Fig. 46 Durham Cathedral, nave interior looking north-east.

Whether or not it is the innovative quadripartite ribbed vaulting and proto-flying buttresses which are the cause of one's visit, the initial response to the cathedral is likely to be to its sheer scale and mass. It is these qualities which have been in the forefront of reactions and evaluations of a host of critics, scholars and travellers from the time of Leland. Its impact on the mind of the early 12th century must have been overwhelming. To judge from the size of extant churches, and from traceable details incorporated in later buildings, the new cathedral would have been many times longer and wider than anything experienced by all but the few travelling elite. Aloft, the ceiling would have astonished, not only by its height – the 70 feet appearing ever higher through the curving lines of the vaulting – but by such height being clad in stone rather than timber. The frame of the west window alone would have been as high as many Saxon churches, while the two dozen paces needed to circle one of the cathedral's massive pillars would have been sufficient to walk the length of the average ecclesiastical building. The cathedral, in short, brought a remarkable scale change in the concept of monumental architecture, certainly in northern Britain.

Setting

Durham is doubly noteworthy in that its innovative architectural features are housed in a remarkable building in a dramatic setting. Engineering achievement is combined with aesthetic quality. The standard two-volume work on Byzantine and Romanesque architecture by Jackson, for instance, describes the stature of the cathedral in the following terms:

> The exterior of Durham, with its three massive towers, its enormous bulk, and its superb position on a rocky promontory round which the river Wear sweeps in a grand wooded defile, makes perhaps the most impressive picture of any cathedral in Europe.[6]

While architects may be drawn to include eulogies over the attractiveness of the building, it is artists who have directly striven to capture, interpret and broadcast its visual beauty. Three centuries and more of sketches and paintings have certified its quality, at the same time enriching and affirming our own appreciation. In more recent times, photography has provided a complementary source, as well as encouraging us, perhaps, to capture our own record.

The aesthetic attraction is evident for all to see, with the interplay of building, site and setting producing a surprising variety of scenic views. Unlike many another cathedral, hemmed in and half-hidden by the built environment, here the domestic respects the monumental, while nature provides a theatrical setting. The myriad of vantage points may be classified by reference to viewpoints first adopted by artists.[7] These may be broadly grouped by their proximity to, and orientation of, the cathedral, which in turn determine the degree of detail shown, the angle of vision and the skyline silhouette. At close quarters, only the view of the south front is interrupted, and that by the former abbey buildings. The other three faces may be admired in full, not least at night when the angled tungsten floodlighting articulates the sculptural detail. At a greater distance, the views incorporating the river, the greenery of the gorge, with perhaps castle and a bridge, form a second grouping; they include the views which Pevsner proclaimed one of the architectural experiences of Europe.[8]

Thirdly, there are the long views, for which Durham has been especially acclaimed. The cathedral is here seen from the rim of the topographical basin in which it is set, rising from the steeply-defined peninsula, with respectful townscape and rolling, green background. Of these, the view from Observatory Field is perhaps the best known, but, working clockwise around the rim, a whole succession of eminences provide vantage points – from Wharton Park, Aykley Heads, Frankland, Gilesgate, Pelaw Woods, Mount Joy, Elvet Hill. In the mid 17th century it was such panoramic views which a Durham prebendary obviously had in mind when, recently returned from a visit to the Holy Land, he likened Durham to Jerusalem.[9]

More dispassionate perhaps, though hardly less complimentary, was the reaction over 200 years later by John Ruskin, when the 19th century painter, architect and formidable critic proclaimed the view from the railway station by Wharton park to be one of the seven wonders of the world.[10] A concluding comment concerning the different settings is that each viewpoint seems to evoke a particular quality of the building – the bulk, strength, drama, romance, majesty and so on.

Symbol

Durham Cathedral is more than innovative, dramatic architecture, it is also significant in cultural terms. Given the co-evolution of church and state, the building can be seen as a political statement; in the words of Trevelyan's *History of England*, it was 'the symbol of the new Latin civilisation brought by the Norman invasion.'[11] Together with the neighbouring castle, it is without parallel as the visible reminder of the Norman conquest of England. It was built as a massive show of strength in the rebellious North and in the broader buffer zone with Scotland. The political significance was confirmed by the institution of a prince bishopric or palatinate, an area stretching from the Tees to the Tweed, in which the bishop of Durham had semi-regal authority, with his own mint, exchequer, parliament, judiciary and army. Well might the poet, then, describe the cathedral as 'Half church of God, half castle 'gainst the Scot.'[12]

The palatinate capitalised on, and succeeded to, the see of St. Cuthbert, originally founded on Lindisfarne in A.D. 635; the new cathedral replaced the Saxon 'White Church' as the shelter for the shrine of the saint, whose body had been borne to Durham by his followers in 995. The building thus assumed the visible mantle of history writ large in the spread of christianity in northern England. An evaluation of its role as an ecclesiastical icon in our own age can be gauged from the response to the threat in the 1940s of a power station barely a mile downriver from the cathedral. The leader columns of *The Times* argued against the economic rationale of the proposal two decades before any national conservation lobby had emerged (see chapter 3).[13] Such a respect for history could, more fundamentally, be interpreted as a feeling for spiritual values. This was the argument of Thomas Sharp in response to the same power station threat:

> Every cathedral city was designed to be a perpetual memorial to the history, continuity, struggles and, in a part anyway, the triumph of the Christian Faith, on which European civilisation is largely founded. So heightened is this function at Durham by nature of the tremendous setting that the question of its mutilation becomes a matter of moment not merely to Durham or Britain but to Christendom.[14]

Defence of the cathedral in the face of a possible power station was not confined to scholars or the elite. Correspondence in local newspapers of the time, for instance, reveals a serviceman, signing himself 'Durham Sapper', writing 'We don't wish to return to find that Big Business has "pulled a fast one" on us while we have been away.'[15] More heart-felt was the 'Miner' from the Blackhall Rocks Company, who felt moved to voice a view contrary to that held, not only by the mine owners, but by his own union leadership:

> Most of us miners are neither chapel nor church-goers, but we have a definite place in our hearts for the majestic loveliness of Durham cathedral. Durham is the miner's haven of peace, his Mecca ... We love to see the stately towers of Durham above the wooded Wear ... I demand, in the interest of the Durham miners, whose sons and brothers have fought and fallen in both wars, that the erection of this power plant be forbidden to pollute the holy atmosphere of Durham.[16]

The stately towers of the cathedral, a focal point on the approach to the city and an orientation guide within, form a dramatic and identifiable skyline silhouette. As a symbol encapsulating the essence of Durham, it attracted a host of artists who both certified, as well as helped create, the icon we know. Their specific vantage points, mentioned earlier, have been used subsequently in a variety of ways; the familiar landmark has long ceased to be the province of high art alone. The depiction of the cathedral on a dozen or so miners' banners, paint on silk, may be considered a transitionary form, as may the posters of the former L.N.E.R. which adorned many a station platform and rail compartment.[17] They are far outnumbered by a host of authorities, businesses and societies which have transformed the silhouette into a graphic symbol. In this realm of booster-imagery – essentially a feature from the 1950s, although first detectable two decades earlier – the towers serve as a civic emblem or logo. At its most extensive, the whole of the pre-Norman kingdom of Northumbria is united under the familiar logo of the three towers (Figure 47). A variety of businesses, in addition, trade under the cathedral name, from bakers and bookshops to travel and videos. Most common, however, postcards and greetings cards apart, is the myriad of household and souvenir items, purchased less perhaps for their intrinsic value than for the picture of the cathedral that they carry.

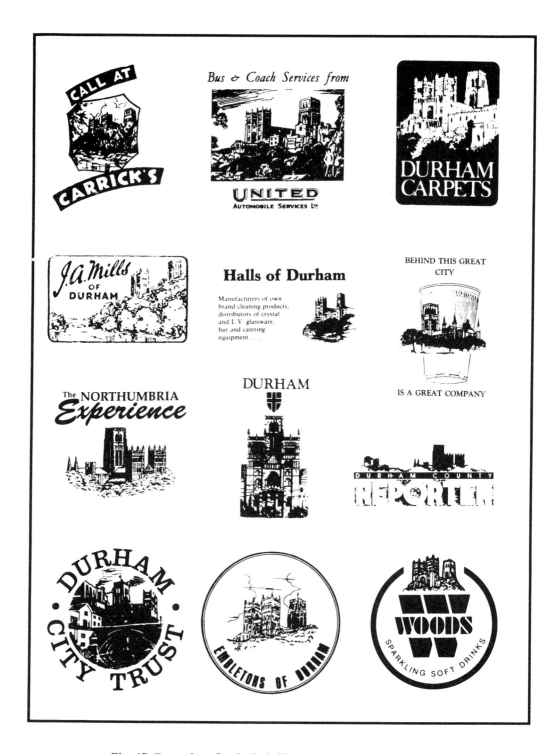

Fig. 47 Examples of cathedral silhouette as an advertising logo.

Conclusion

The ultimate distinctiveness of Durham Cathedral as 'the best building in the world' stems from the fact that it witnesses to a story: that architecture and aesthetics point to the Norman confirmation of an earlier history and Saxon saint. The existing Norman structure represents time locked-up, a gigantic pause in the temporal flow of history. At the same time, in Eliot's phrase, one is aware in Durham of the presence, as well as the pastness of the past, for the story is kept alive, celebrated, enacted daily, weekly, annually by its clerics along with citizens, scholars, miners and a host of other regional and diocesan groups, as well as by modern pilgrims. In short, it is the incarnation of our existence.

7   The Galilee Chapel: Sacred Space

Guidebook Summary

The Galilee Chapel. Built circa 1175-1180 by Bishop Hugh of Le Puiset at the west end of Durham Cathedral forty years after completion of the main building. Part of World Heritage Site. 23 metres wide and 15 metres long, divided internally into five aisles, each four bays in length. Late Romanesque, with some Transitional motifs. Round-headed arches, heavily chevroned, on slender quatrefoil piers with twin sandstone and limestone shafts. 14th century windows in north and south walls, 15th century in west; small panels of medieval glass recently reinstated. Medieval wall paintings in and above altar recess and on arcade of inner northern aisle. Original entrance, the great west door of cathedral, blocked by the central altar and chantry tomb of Bishop Langley (1406-37), who provided replacement flanking doors to both north and south. Plain, marble tomb-chest of Venerable Bede, 1370, in southern inner aisle. See Figure 48.

Place Evocation

The Galilee is architectural space, but its appreciation lies beyond any succinct guidebook statement. Appreciation begins with the fact that the chapel stands in contrast to the major church of which it is part and through which it is entered. It is not the cathedral writ small. The cathedral is a massive display of Norman strength, the chapel an exercise in the delicate. One, patriarchal, the other feminine, truly a Lady Chapel. In one, William of St Calais[1] demonstrated to the world how to clad the heavens in stone; that proven, Hugh of Le Puiset[2] abandoned thrust-withstanding structures and, in place of pillars that measure two dozen paces round, substituted shafts as slender as a ballerina's waist. (The contrast as originally conceived was even more emphatic than is apparent today, for abaci and bases of the Galilee indicate Puiset's design daringly proposed that the triple-banded chevron arches would be upheld by a series of separate twin shafts - as shown by the westernmost pairs - and not by fusions of four.)

The increased proportion of window to wall admits a light which emphasizes both a delicacy of sculptural form and purity of stone, not least that forming the regular mathematical stonework of the spandrels. (The stone here provides few examples of iron-stained swirls which warm some other parts of the cathedral.) There is no need to supplement the lighting by clerestory openings, but mouldings on outer arcade spandrels suggest it was considered an option until a late stage in the construction. Although the architectural evidence appears incontrovertible, we do well to remind ourselves that the original decision was taken in lighting conditions different from those which prevail today from Early English and Perpendicular fenestration.

It is the Galilee's quality of light which may beckon in the first instance, out of the grey of the nave, especially after noon and most particularly when the low evening rays of the sun irradiate the whole interior. It is in the summer evening sun that Christ the Morning Star

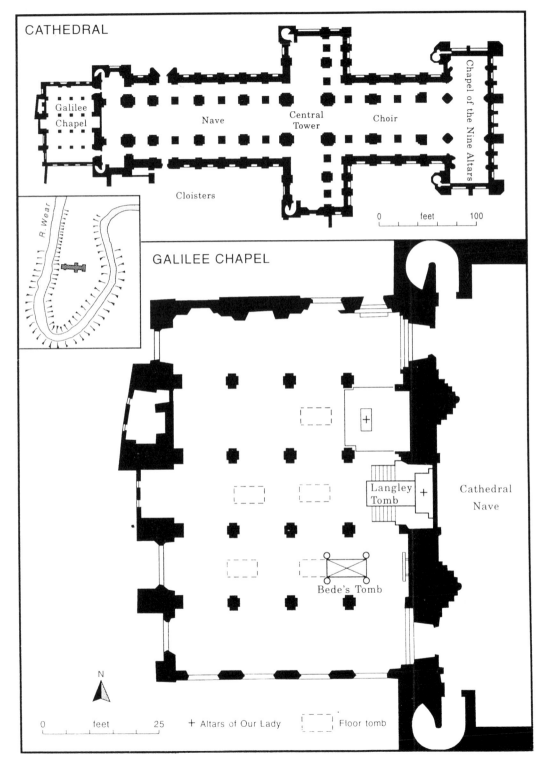

CATHEDRAL

Galilee
Chapel

Nave

Central
Tower

Choir

Chapel of the Nine Altars

Cloisters

0   feet   100

R. Wear

GALILEE CHAPEL

Langley
Tomb

Cathedral
Nave

Bede's Tomb

N

0   feet   25   + Altars of Our Lady   Floor tomb

Fig. 48 Lay-out plan of Galilee Chapel.

63

blazes apocalyptically from the gilt lettering of Bede's commentary,[3] thereby proclaiming the role of this particular architectural space.

The quality of light encourages some to perceive a Moorish influence to this arcaded hall. The initial glance of the interior is certainly across the receding planes of deeply-chevroned arches springing from one slender cluster of columns to the next. This first impression may well prove to be the lasting one - less perhaps because of the special value attaching to first encounters, more attributable to the space having no single focal point. It is diffuse architectural space, which may be read as if it were a gallery. The building is wider than it is long - almost as wide as the cathedral itself and much wider than its nave - and has no west door from which the eye may focus eastwards. Where such a door might be is a low and deeply-recessed window. (A glance through that beaded window explains all, for the chapel perches at the very edge of the river gorge. Inside, several glass 'tell-tales', all dated 12:61, are modern checks by structural engineers that Langley's four external buttresses are still clamping the building to the rock.) Entry to the chapel is, in fact, *from* the east, *from* the Christian stage, so that the sought-for orientation is back over our shoulder. We have, therefore, initially to move away, before turning to acknowledge, and approach, the altar. - But which one?

At the east end of the tallest, central aisle the dark altar and shielded monument of Bishop Langley thrust forward into the chapel from the recess of the cathedral's great west portal. The Westphalian/Spanish triptych[4] softens and distracts - not least the puzzling golden birds in stylised flight, which on closer inspection, recede into the three painted scenes as haloes. The 16th century artist has been undone by context, for here raised triptych and low angle of reflected light combine to thwart the subtlety intended in the use of gold leaf: the ethereal becomes earthly, the mysterious, amusing. But there can be no disguising of the great portal behind. (Did ever such intimate space have such a massive door?) The prominence of the original entrance is punctuated by the recessed series of chevroned semicircles, which lock cog-like either side into the rhythmic movement of aisle arcades approaching at right angles, the whole resembling the upper portion of a gigantic clockwork mechanism in stone. (It is the thrust of this unifying and boldly Romanesque architectural element which proclaims the political authority of state and church militant. If the zig-zag patterning is described as dog-tooth chevron, then the new metaphor releases the snarl of bared teeth to stir memories of the Harrying of the North[5] brought by the Conquest and to remind onlookers that the pride of Saxon building had been erased to make way for the Norman cathedral. At the same time, the tension of heavy Romanesque and delicate Early English appears to echo the colourful, talented but scheming patron prince-bishop, one time Regent of All England).

The unifying rhythm of chevroned semicircle was later respected by Bishop Langley in his design over a new south entrance, although over the equivalent north entrance he perversely dropped oval for pointed arch. This feature may not be immediately apparent, since the eye's quest for symmetry is thwarted more immediately in the aisles flanking the Langley altar. To the right, the sculptural gilt lettering of Bede's text on an oak screen contrasts with the venerable scholar's plain, black tomb, detached from the east wall and projecting lengthwise into the chapel. Four Florentine candlesticks stand sentinel-like, one at each corner, with a dark prayer-desk at the end for the lone pilgrim. To the left, rows of pews, stretching back from a light oak altar rail, occupy much of the aisle. It is the furniture, and not the apparently plain east wall, which announces that here is the expected point of present activity, if not attention.

*

'The Lord is here.'
'His spirit is with us.'

At the early morning celebration the folds of the chasuble on the outstretched arms of the priest conform to and complete the painted drapery of the medieval artist on the east wall before him. The small congregation present is not here to verify, instruct themselves, or inform curiosity... they are here to kneel, for this is a holy place. Holiness is incarnated in the Galilee from centuries of this central ritual, not only at one of the two altars of Our Lady, but also at that of St. Bede or Holy Cross. Its presence is further witnessed by the bones of a venerable saint, and more generally reinforced by an iconography which closely replicates that of the cathedral itself. At the chief altar of the Lady Chapel the medieval depictions of Cuthbert[6] and Oswald[7] on the jambs of the recess originally faced toward a central statue of the Virgin, thereby echoing the three central figures of the Neville screen at the nave high altar; the tomb of St Bede balances that of St Cuthbert behind the high altar - both once glorious shrines, both now dressed in post-Reformation sobriety; the chantry of Langley is the equivalent of Hatfield's[8] in the chancel.

Holy space induces stillness, quiet, and invites us to linger. In time, eyes that saw not are slowly opened and decipher colourful stones where once there were grey. Most notably aloft, the south wall arcading of the north aisle is busy with a central crucifixion scene, flanked by other depictions of disciples being variously crucified, beheaded, boiled in oil or flayed. On the spandrel nearest the altar is a more tranquil scene of three Durham monks in Benedictine habit, praying. Above the eastern recess of this, the only aisle to have such painted figure-subjects, experts can see a huge painting of the Coronation of the Virgin. But by now, we ourselves have a vision which can detect traces of a former widespread architectural polychromy - painted masonry patterns above the arcades, outline chevrons on roll mouldings or arches, colouring on abaci of capitals.

If change of fashion in a former era caused the general removal of colour, it is wear and tear which has worn and levelled the floor tombs dotted about the Galilee. The most notable exception is that of Mrs Dorothy Greye, wife to Henry Greye Esquire: she died May 21 Anno Domini 1662, and is capped by a slab of Frosterley marble[9] with a topography sufficiently strong to deter casual, irreverent trespassing. It is unfortunate that respect for Mrs Greye may take one over the adjacent and reliefless tomb of John Brimley, who, it is worthily recorded, 'By musickes heavenlie harmonie, Dull minds he maid in God rejoice'.

65

(Adjacent features today, the tombs in fact bestride the Reformation, for the inspirer of dull minds was the last monastic cantor.)

Erosion - and colour - of a different kind is revealed by the Galilee's other limestone which we fondly term marble, the Purbeck stone, which constitutes the darker pair of shafts in each cluster. Their single bedding planes, highly polished by medieval masons, are now heavily stained and savagely pock-marked, chemical warfare having been spearheaded by sulphuric acid when coke-heaters were introduced in more recent times. A different chemical make-up of the twin sandstone shafts allowed them to survive unscathed, although they have provided an easier target for human imprint. Thus, JN was here in 1770, WT in 1799; R.L. March was at an adjacent rear pillar, while SB, TR and a tall HH, all in modern-face Roman, were to the right of Bede's tomb. In every instance the visiting card was left on the west side of the pillar, probably signifying more an eye on the alert than on the altar. (Whether coincidence or not, it is interesting to reflect that this particular activity occurred during an era of official stone chiselling and redressing. During the 1790s, moreover, the chapel was on the list of proposed demolitions by the cathedral's so-called 'improvers'.)

In a few places the sandstone has yielded to natural erosion. Some of the pier bases - unlike the capitals - have lost much definition and are dust-coloured, if not dust-like. By a similar process the piscine to the left of the north-most altar has blurred and regressed to assume a form not seen since early in its carving. Below the Bede gilt screen, the lowest course of sandstone is worn and strangely rubble-like. Reflecting that the Galilee was built outside the west end of the cathedral, and at a lower level, it is almost as if part of the great church's foundations are exposed. Surely not! In marked contrast is the Frosterley marble of the Langley altar: a dark slice through a fossilised aquarium, as clearly written as when first laid down in the former limestone sea.

Time, then, is locked in this place, but its passage is also recorded. Its presence, whether of still-stand or passage, contributes to a spirit of reflection and quiet, for the Galilee is aside from the eventful mainstream of the cathedral. Aside and holy, but not aloof - quiet but not silent - for from the nave is carried the muffled buzz of busyness, punctuated perhaps by a child finding its echo, the twice-daily cascade of cash from offertory box emptying, an organ tuning or a dismembered voice crisply, if faintly, relaying the spoken word of mattins and evensong from a concealed speaker. Throughout the round of these happenings, the decibel measure in the Galilee may be no higher than the rustle of a verger's cassock in rhythmic beat to the rub of trouser and forward-tap by rubber-soled shoe.

*

"San Bede ē chiamato venerabile perchē durante la sua vita si ē comportato come un Santo, dimostrando inoltre una saggezza e una cultura notevoli. Egli ē stato commemorato da Dante Alighieri. Qui vediamo una delle preghiere del Venerabile San Bede tradotta dal latino ...."

It is 12.30 on Tuesday. Every Tuesday at this time in the season an Italian party is gathered by Bede's tomb in the Galilee; half an hour earlier a party of Germans stood here; yet to come are groups from Spain, France and, perhaps Greece. Each group leader, equipped with brolly for party cohesion as much as weather, drops a distant countenance during his or her sudden, brief exposition. No question defeats - not that there is time for considered discussion, for the chapel is but part of the cathedral, and the cathedral but part of today's itinerary.

Such bands of pilgrims from foreign lands may not tarry long or be here to kneel, but in verifying, informing curiosity and carrying report, they authenticate history and the Galilee as a holy place. Enrichment comes no less from the occasional, more leisurely local group, addressed by a cathedral bedesman;[10] they are seated, he anecdotal. More intent are those guidebook individuals or couples who, having followed the two stars to Durham cathedral, logically complete the worthwhile journey by taking in the single star rating of the Galilee. With nose in guidebook, and with an eye seeking to confirm, they alone may mount the seven steps to the Langley altar or step inside the altar rail to inspect medieval artwork, all in a process to certify others' knowledge. Those without advantage of the latter may dismiss the Galilee with summary glance from the doorway, dismissal presumably based on the view of the rear wall: a blank frame in a flickering image. Alternatively, and given less haste, they may be diverted by their own findings - the noticeboard illustrating the diocesan link with Lesotho, the floor tomb of Mrs Dorothy Greye, the view from the back window, or, for children, perhaps even the central heating bunkers. Those with neither knowledge nor inquisitiveness may promenade the circuit from door round to door, hands in pocket, camera on navel, minds elsewhere, their bodies in no place. 'Shall we go upstairs now, or shall we have a look at the shops?'

*

The Galilee: palimpsest in time, place of anamnesis. Time-thickened yet thin, a focus of happenings, a locus where structure, fabric, organisation, use, evaluation, meaning are endlessly challenged, changed, continued. At the intersection of this timeless moment is the Lady Mass, rendered daily by the Song School and echoed further by the Langley Mass and Holy Cross celebration. On Sundays monks voice their sermons from an iron pulpit, while the cathedral's great processions end here. The chancellor from his throne before clerks and litigants dispenses the temporal authority of his Lord Bishop - land transactions, appeals, petitions, writs, pardons. 'Judicium Jehovae es ...', though faded, still speaks from above the portal of this consistory court, but not of the diocesan registry also here.

'Why not convert the space into a divinity school?' asks Archdeacon Thorp.[11] As a prison, the captive Scottish militia from Dunbar[12] search frantically for timber to warm seventeenth century frozen limbs. Nineteenth-century undergraduates complain at having to attend morning prayer, hardly less at having to breathe sulphurous fumes at the same time. What did Humphry Davy recommend?[13]

Fig. 49 Galilee Chapel.

The production of 'Jesus Christ, Superstar' blinds and deafens; the low ceiling bounces back the band's decibels. Wyatt[14] acts to remove the roof, Salvin[15] moves the Langley altar to open the great portal. Both are frustrated. The chantry's sides are dismantled, a triptych and screen appear. Stained glass is smashed, fragments are pieced together and reinstated. Colour is whitewashed, parts of the polychromy are exhumed.

A sudden flash photograph is taken, although notices clearly forbid it. JN, 1770. WT, 1799. 'Are you the custodian?' An elder child brings a shriek of joy to his little brother by threatening to wheel him at speed down the entrance ramp. The child of excommunicated parents cries during its baptism. The lungs of a Saga group make their complaint, while the owners give voice to aching feet. 'Are you sketching?' One of the four bells of the 'Galilee Steeple' rings to announce a fugitive at the North Door has claimed sanctuary. Pairs of school-children buzz around after each other, eager to be first to complete their class competition. A monk in grey habit kneels at Bede's prayer desk.

For the last half-hour of the day the Galilee and I are alone, sharing the silence of centuries, sharing the history of centuries and hours that have happened but not completely unhappened. Soon the curfew bell will toll. I am the custodian. I am sketching.

Afterword

My sketching of the Galilee extends over two decades; I have been engaged on a personal odyssey, compiling a personal diary. Discourse and text have thus been a personal affair, representing a struggle to give outward expression to a myriad of inner feelings and promptings. I have looked with mine ears, observing, absorbing its story and observing again. Architecture, action and atmosphere have been imbibed - severally, successively, simultaneously. I have been uplifted by the lightness of pillar, cowed under the weight of history; been solicitous of crumbling sandstone, fortified by mouldering saints' bones; felt at home in it, proprietorial towards it; taken it for granted, knelt in awe in it, admired it as theatre and scenery. Through such dialectic and signification have I observed the Galilee, been its custodian, imagined it, created, built it. The Galilee is my world.

My sketching represents personal experience of coming to know through understanding, but understanding gained reciprocally: the world gave itself to me in so far as I opened myself to it. The result of such sharing is a social construction. I am part of a common humanity, sharing a particular culture and language; the Galilee, in turn is a world suspended in the webs of significance spun over eight centuries. I have therefore swum in the stream of history, becoming increasing aware of others' actions and reactions. The diversity of observed engagements, reflecting a spectrum of visitor yearnings, are the most recent skeins in the web of place-making. The Galilee is a shared world.

The Galilee is my world, a shared world, but in the beginning there was the Galilee. When I first entered the chapel, ignorant if expectant, it was a world already complete. Acquaintance brought an increasingly rich, meaningful and loved world into focus: it was I who was changed and made richer. Before I was, the Galilee is. The chapel was less an object for a subject, more a subject to which I was happily subject. The relationship was thus one of waiting on the subject, allowing the chapel to disclose itself on its terms, in its time. In a process where paradox ever lurks, it is as if the personal, freed from considering the subjective as a burden, results in a text which is neither an act of ventriloquism by the author nor of advocacy, but rather of amanuensis. As a consequence, the emergent text is a translation or interpretation, the success of which is to be assessed by the extent to which it conveys, convinces or authenticates a sense of being there. A comparison of word and world is the challenge, then - to both author and reader.

Notes

1. William of St. Calais (or Carileph), the second Norman bishop of Durham, 1081-96. During his bishopric the Saxon cathedral was pulled down and the present building begun in 1093.

2. Hugh of Le Puiset, the sixth Norman bishop of Durham, 1153-95, was an active builder within the city and beyond. He was Co-Regent of All England during King Richard I's absence abroad on the Third Crusade.

3. The remains of the Venerable Bede (674-735) of Jarrow Monastery, biblical scholar and historian, were transferred to the Saxon cathedral in 1022 and placed in the

Galilee Chapel in 1370. The quotation was incorporated in 1970 on a monument to Dean Alington and wife designed by George Pace.

4. The triptych, three painted panels of the crucifixion and dated c. 1500 from Westphalia (north-west Germany), was given to the cathedral in 1935.

5. The Harrying, or laying waste of the countryside, was ordered by William the Conqueror in 1070, to avenge the massacre in the city of Robert Cumin and his retinue, who had been sent north by the king to take control of Northumbria.

6. St. Cuthbert (634-87), north of England's most famous saint. His body was brought to Durham by the Lindisfarne or Cuthbert Community in 995. The cathedral, built to contain his shrine, was dedicated to the saint until the Reformation.

7. St. Oswald (604-42), King of Northumbria, invited Aidan to Lindisfarne as a base from which to convert the North of England to christianity. He was killed fighting the pagan King of Mercia.

8. Thomas Hatfield, Bishop of Durham 1345-81, built an elaborate chantry, surmounted by an episcopal throne, on the south side of the chancel.

9. The deposit, named after a village in Weardale, is not technically a 'marble', but a hard, dark, heavily fossiliferous Lower Carboniferous Limestone.

10. A bedesman is a uniformed, honorary verger.

11. Charles Thorp, Archdeacon of Durham and subsequently first warden of the University, for which he was a prime mover. In 1831 he unsuccessfully proposed that the Galilee Chapel should become the divinity school of the university.

12. In late 1650 the cathedral served as a prison for 3,000 Scottish soldiers, brought south after Cromwell's victory at the battle of Dunbar.

13. Sir Humphrey Davy, inventor of the miner's safety lamp, was brought in to investigate the chemical weathering of the chapel's Purbeck marble columns; the deterioration was attributed to fumes from coke braziers.

14. James Wyatt, invited by the chapter in 1795 to submit plans for improvements to the cathedral, recommended demolition of the Galilee Chapel. Lead was actually removed from the chapel roof in 1796, before a public outcry caused the work to cease.

15. Anthony Salvin (1799-1881), London-based architect of Durham origin, opened the West Door in 1845 in order to restore the original Norman vista. The result was disappointing, and so the door was re-sealed and the Langley altar replaced.

8   The View from Prebends' Bridge: Landscape and Memory

In 1778 the Dean and Chapter of Durham completed a new stone bridge across the river Wear to replace an earlier one destroyed by floods at the beginning of the decade. The siting of the new Prebends' Bridge, named after the cathedral prebendaries or canons, was some fifty metres further downstream and thus clear of the southern loop in the incised meander of the river. It therefore opened up a classical prospect of cathedral and castle amid the wooded slopes or 'Banks' of the gorge, which several decades earlier had been landscaped by its ecclesiastical owners for the benefit of promenaders. The new prospect from Prebends' Bridge was soon to become a highlight, perhaps *the* acclaimed point, from which to view the peninsular acropolis. A succession of artists was attracted (see chapter 2). Turner's rendering of the scene in 1835, included in his *Picturesque Views in England and Wales* project,[1] is shown in Figure 12.

Acclaim, and dissemination, of this valued landscape has not, however, been confined to landscape aesthetes, for a variety of publications and products, souvenirs and postcards carry the well-known view. And for every artist, there have been thousands of ordinary visitors or tourists, many of them 'moved' to capture the scene, not in pencil or paint, but on film. The present essay focuses on introspection by respondents as they anticipate, and then compare, their photographic record with the experience 'alive' in memory. In theoretical terms the exercise was conducted in the knowledge of the broad characteristics of memory as outlined in psychological texts, where, briefly, remembering is shown to be a process of reconstruction, not reproduction. Memory retains, but it does so selectively by simplifying, by forgetting what we do not need or perhaps want to remember, by re-ordering, so that greater coherence may be created than was actually present on location.

The research design involved capturing respondents after they had taken a photograph on the spot approximating to the prospect adopted in Turner's painting, that is, near to Sir Walter Scott's plaque at the western end of the bridge. (Those adding persons as foreground or choosing vantage points elsewhere on the bridge were ignored.) The view, according to the author's camera, is given in Figure 50. In order to minimize variation in viewing conditions, fieldwork was confined to between mid-morning and mid-afternoon on sunny July and August days.[2] All respondents were on holiday, and mostly for a period, although a few were on a day's outing. Of the hundred photographers captured, 49 completed the subsequent stages of the project by returning questionnaires designed to test and compare photographic record with memory recall.

The Photograph Anticipated

The first of two sealed envelopes taken and opened away from Durham requested respondents to anticipate their photograph by sketching, within a supplied frame, the outline of the main features which they expected their photograph would show. Bearing in mind the exact position from which the photograph had been taken – which factor determined respondent selection in the first instance – a variation of two prospects was

71

Fig. 50 The View from Prebends' Bridge (Author's camera).

expected, depending on exact camera angle. In fact three prospects emerged (Table 6). The expected, fuller view, incorporating cathedral, river and part of the distant medieval Framwellgate Bridge (Figure 51 a, b) was selected by nearly half, a further quarter drew a more restricted version by omitting the bridge and producing a cathedral-focused sketch (51 c,d). Interestingly, the bulk of drawings in this group exaggerated the size of the cathedral, many simulating the result of a telephoto lens (which they did not use). The remaining quarter, however, drew an unexpected variant, given the specific viewpoint or origin: a bridge-focused sketch, with the river, between symmetrical banks, focusing with narrowing perspective on a centrally-positioned Framwellgate Bridge (51 e, f). A moment's reflection suggests that such a view will have been seen from the middle of the bridge, which was traversed by all but a few respondents. The precise photographic spot has therefore been subsumed within the overall experience of the bridge. Within this more general recall, the inherent good figure tendency of the memory has encouraged a simplified, more symmetrical product, a finding well attested from mental mapping exercises.

	Respondents		
Prospect	Home (N=33)	Overseas (N=16)	Total (N=49)
Cathedral and part-Bridge	13	10	23
Cathedral-focused	7	6	13
Bridge-focused	13	0	13

Table 6: The three prospects of sketches anticipating the photographed view.

A break-down of sketch-types between British and overseas respondents reveals a significant variation. Bearing in mind the different population sizes, it can be seen that the latter favour cathedral-bridge and cathedral prospects, while the bridge focus derives entirely from home respondents. Explanation is not immediately obvious. That foreigners may be more cathedral-orientated is perhaps acceptable, given the observed wider possession of touring guide books, and therefore more likely knowledge of the architectural and historical significance of the cathedral.

When commenting on content inaccuracy, as opposed to error in prospect or graphic inability, it should be emphasized that the drawings represent sketches of anticipated photographic realism, not artistic impressions of landscape experience, with all the subjective licence that this alternative implies. The results suggest however that the two are not mutually exclusive.

In one-fifth of the drawings, especially those with a cathedral-focus prospect, the cathedral is much more prominent than it is in reality from the Prebends' Bridge vantage point. Figure 51c,d well illustrates the point. Only a telephoto lens and a position downstream at river level – plus a lowering of the gorge! – could have achieved this effect. The same applies to the sketch in Figure 51b, except that here an aerial view has been adopted. The foreshortening permits details of both foreground (boating, willows, 'seat') and background (car on bridge, although in fact this is a false projection, for the eye at Prebends' Bridge was deceived in that the bridge carrying vehicular traffic is farther downstream, hidden by Framwellgate Bridge).

A quarter of the sketches misjudge the number of cathedral towers, the majority depicting just two, although five opt for a single one. A recall of but part of the general experience, whereby the towers emerge and grow in stature as one crosses the bridge, may offer an explanation, although this would not account for the four who recalled pepper-pot spires rather than towers.

Nearly one in five wrongly remembered the number of arches of Framwellgate Bridge, all but one showing three, rather than two. The three arches of Prebends' Bridge itself, or perhaps the multiple arches of Durham's other medieval bridge, may be conflated within the memory of the sketches. – Or perhaps three makes for better symmetry than two, for all but two of the examples were on bridge-focused projections. A few exaggerated the depth of gorge incision, while one was so overwhelmed by the foliage and sunny weather that Framwellgate Bridge is omitted, the river disappearing into a forest of trees, while the sun shines down from the northern sky on frolicking boatmen.

The Photograph Received

With the photograph of the scene eventually to hand, a further set of unseen questions sought respondent reaction to the received picture before a more general appraisal of memory and experience. The loss of one photograph in processing meant

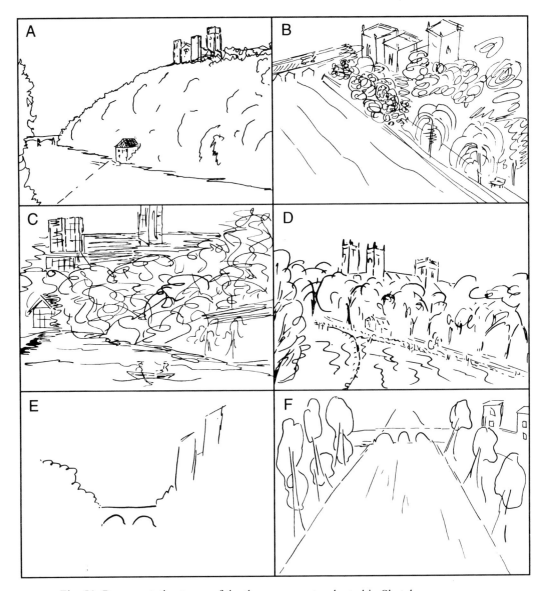

Fig. 51 Representative types of the three prospects adopted in Sketches
anticipating the photographed view from Prebends' Bridge: A, B – Cathedral
and Bridge; C, D – Cathedral-focused; E, F – Bridge-focused.

there was one fewer respondent at this stage.

The extent to which the major elements in the valued landscape varied in prominence compared with the remembered scene is summarised in percentage form in Table 7. To a degree, the different reactions correlate with the two contributing populations. Thus, with home visitors the river and bridge had been disproportionately large in memory – it will be remembered that bridge-focused sketches were confined to British respondents – whereas the cathedral had been mentally reduced in prominence such as to evoke surprise on receipt of photograph. In contrast, overseas visitors carried the reverse image, such that the photograph did not record the dominance which the cathedral had enjoyed in memory, where it had clearly been 'larger than life'. Again, it will be remembered that cathedral-focused sketches had been twice as frequent among the overseas population. Consistent with what was perhaps a more emphatic historic focus among foreign visitors, the castle also figured more prominently in the memory, also the ancient millhouse. As a result, the river and trees were now shown by the photograph to be more prominent than were remembered.

	Cathedral		Castle		River		Trees		Bridge		Mill	
	+	-	+	-	+	-	+	-	+	-	+	-
Home	44	22	9	6	9	22	17	6	0	47	0	17
Overseas	0	50	0	25	19	0	31	13	0	13	0	19
TOTAL	29	31	2	13	13	15	21	8	0	35	0	17

Table 7. Elements more (+) or less (-) prominent on respondent photograph compared with memory. (% of sketches)

One final feature to be mentioned from the detailed comparison of memory and photographs are the new elements among the 'surprise inclusions' on respondents' photographs. Whether it be the directed eye in the field or the subsequent act of remembering, the few young willows and the grassed area in the right foreground had been overlooked. Attention was presumably on the view and the focus long-distance. Similarly, the people, captured on photograph but unnoticed at the time, had obviously been 'invisible' to the eye captivated by a 'natural' scene.

Assessment of Photograph and Memory

The invitation to comment generally on a comparison between photographic record and memory of experience of the scene elicited a strong emphasis on the richness of the latter (Table 8). Even in visual terms the evidence of the photograph was considered deficient, the first-hand experience having been three-dimensional, offering a 'wider view' with 'no vertical or horizontal limits to the vision'. The photograph in contrast was 'totally unable to convey the life of the scene'; unable to discriminate, it merely 'recorded

Visual		Non-visual		Experiential	
Movement	14	Smells	7	Atmosphere	13
Colour	9	Feel	7	Personal Involvement	7
Wider view	9	Sounds	5	Drama	4
3-dimensional	7			Circumstantial	4
Fuller, richer	4				
Sunshine	4				
Texture	3				

Table 8. Additional qualities of memory of experience compared with photographic records (Totals of respondent comments)

everything' at 'one instant'. Experience, and the memory of that experience, are 'quite otherwise'. The respondent who noted, 'The eye, and the memory, register selectively, and my memory proved to be a collection of impressions from a number of visits', was articulating a further reason for the richness of memory. Namely, in compressing time, the memory distils the essence by anchoring spatially events which were temporally separate.

Experience was also remembered as more colourful and more full of texture, besides the incorporation of movement. 'Memory is not a still life', recorded one respondent, and thus the flow of the river, motion of boats, the breeze and people contribute life to the scene.

In non-visual terms, the memory retains sounds of water (the breaking of water over the downstream weir), birds, rustling leaves and, perhaps, even silence. (In reality, silence is a later projection onto the scene, the eye having dominated the ear on location, and memory having completed the conspiracy). The senses of smell (of leaves, bushes, plants, even water) and touch (the warmth, the breeze, the well-matured stone of the bridge) also contribute to the richness.

Apart from a richness emanating from the basic senses, both visual and non-visual, memory incorporates a much wider group of recalls which may be collectively termed experiential. It incorporates, first, the general atmosphere of peace, 'the feeling of history', 'the sense of cathedral dominance', and so on. Then, there is decided drama, set by the dense foliage of the river gorge and realized by stepping out into the open across the bridge. 'The actual experience was more outstanding owing to suddenly viewing the cathedral and river together, which is a feeling that cannot be recorded by photo', is a home visitor's summary; 'coming out of nowhere' is a shorter description of the dramatic appearance of the cathedral.

A sense of personal involvement is also important – of 'actually being there', 'being in the centre of it' or, more intimately, 'actually being part of the whole scene', 'being an "integral part" of the scene rather than an outside observer', as two home visitors noted. The photograph, in contrast, definitely does 'not convey the awareness of being part of the whole scene as when actually standing on the bridge'.

The context, or circumstance, also colours the memory. Apart from feel ('lovely to be on holiday'), company can well add to or detract from the actual experience. Witness the following from a London visitor:

> When I was on the bridge I was showing the cathedral to a friend, who was seeing it for the first time. Her appreciation and my enthusiasm made it a rich experience. It is now enshrined in memory and could not be caught on film. That is a mere aid, not a reality. The shared experience of that lovely day will not be forgotten.

That we see through others' eyes is well known, but this example illustrates that the influence is not in one direction, for the newcomer, in bringing fresh vision to a scene, can stir new life into an old scene, rekindling something of that unrepeatable sensation of our first encounter.

Memory stores and keeps the experience alive, in which process the photograph is an aid, 'a souvenir'. The Canadian who, while on the bridge, volunteered that the picture was 'taken for memory when I leave', illustrates the point, albeit in North American tourist fashion. 'One of my roses for December' is perhaps a more poetic reference to its souvenir quality. Thus, although 'more definite' or 'more objective', the photograph remains 'an aid, not a reality'. Reality lives in the memory, for which the photograph is a trigger, a trigger both for a wider area than the view recorded and for reliving the richer experience. Two comments from overseas visitors illustrate this dual point. The photograph of a South African was considered 'an aid to prompt memory of the occasion of my visit to Durham city and particularly the cathedral'; to an Austrian 'the photograph can reproduce a feeling that I had once and can make me feel grateful'.

The memory, then, is 'a collection of impressions'. It is 'not a still life' but 'moves and lives', so that at each recollection the cathedral might be experienced anew as 'coming out of nowhere'. It is richer, in time becoming perhaps 'more dreamlike' such that, as one French visitor found, 'the photo puts limits to my imagination'. An Australian carried the process further: 'In a sense, memory and the recalled experience become independent of the view itself'. It was very much of a lone voice, therefore, and a dedicated photographer, who insisted that 'By its accuracy a photo corrects memory. The photo I have is more pleasing artistically than my memory of the scene.'

Discussion of Landscape in Memory

The subjectivity of remembering is clearly evident in the present exercise, with the anticipatory sketches and reaction to actual photographs providing simple measures of the extent to which the remembrance of the valued landscape differed from the apparent accuracy of the camera. The sketches are interesting in that, although the exercise was one of anticipating photographic objectivity, yet the memory clearly induced the subjectivity of the artist. Thus, apart from errors in detail to the cathedral towers or numbers or arches in Framwellgate Bridge, the very size of the cathedral and, in a few cases, the depth of the gorge, may be interpreted as errors of an entirely different kind. Indeed they are hardly errors at all if they are seen as correctly conveying to the respondent the impressiveness and significance of the object – the essence of the scene – as experienced on location and subsequently melded in memory. Such an interpretation is considered valid even though the fitting of a scene within a camera's framehold is hardly the same interpretative exercise as the artist's study of composition. The present respondent-photographers were themselves artists in that, apart from the quickly taken – and, aptly-named – snaps, they spent a considerably longer time on the bridge, viewing the landscape and reflecting upon it in silence or with a companion and, of course, with the investigator. In short, they were imbibing the essence of place and the stuff of which memories are made.

It is instructive if one turns from the artists of the present exercise to the views from Prebends' Bridge as recorded by a succession of past painters and other professional sketchers. A comparison interestingly brings to light errors of detail similar to those in the sketches of respondents here – details in cathedral towers, number of arches in the distant bridge, even the direction of river flow in one instance! Such inaccuracies prompt questions into rules of composition, of relation of artist to the scene and of relation between artist and subsequent intervening engraver or illustrator. But, more fundamental than errors caused by such variables are the conscious distortions incurred for the sake of spirit or essence of place. A supreme example of such a work, of a memory made visible, is the painting of the scene by J.M.W. Turner (See page 25 and Figure 12).

If minor details of error are ignored, the major distortion for the benefit of truth in Turner's painting is the elevating and turning of the cathedral some forty-five degrees. All lines lead to this central focus, not least the bridge parapet in the foreground, which is a further piece of artistic licence. The poetry in the scene may have lingered long in the inward eye, for the painting was executed in 1835, well over three decades after the first of several visits to Durham.

Given the subjectivity of memory as outlined, then we can appreciate the comment of the art historian Friedlander that 'our need of verisimilitude is not satisfied by photography'.[3] C. Day Lewis, in a discussion of the poetic image, assessed even colour photography to be 'flat and unreal', its objectivity being perhaps better described as a 'dead accuracy'.[4] (The reader is invited to compare Figures 12 and 50). Most respondents in the present exercise made comments which concurred with the assessment of finding the experience and memory superior to the photograph. Two of the fullest articulations came from overseas visitors, the first from New Zealand and the second from Canada.

> I'm not disappointed in my photo, it came out well, but the memory of standing on the bridge is much fuller. The photo shows none of the Prebends' Bridge, which the memory of the experience includes. The motion of people and boats and water, and the warmth of the sun are all part of the memory not

included in the picture. The memory moves and lives, but the photo is stopped at an instant.

And,

> Of course I would say that the actual experience is (or was) richer than the photograph, the photograph after all being only a two-dimensional reproduction of the real thing. But I think I would have to say that even my memories are more impressive than the photograph as well. This raises some very interesting questions in my own mind, therefore, about just why I bother taking photographs.

Few may have shared, or been aware of, the dilemma expressed at the end of the second quotation, for, despite the popularity of photography, it could be argued that the camera lens is merely the Claude glass of a previous century, such that it is easy to look but more difficult to see. Yet it is the very quality of seeing that is the basis of memory, a precious companion which has been shown to be at once both selective and collective in origin, dominated by the eye yet sensory-rich, error-prone yet truthful. Hence the validity, as exemplified by the present study, of considering landscape less a physical object, more an extension of the mind.

9   The Upper Room Sculpture: A Trompe L'œil in a City of Illusions

Introduction

In the 1980s Dutch elm disease led to the selective culling of trees on the banks of the River Wear in its incised meander loop around the peninsula. One unusual feature to stem from this event was the assembling and carving of thirteen of the mature elm trunks into a highly distinctive piece of public art. The sculptor was Colin Wilbourn, Cathedral Artist in residence, 1986-87. The sculpture, called The Upper Room, is sited on a level area near to Prebends' Bridge at the southernmost part of the river loop. The trunks are arranged in a long oval, staking out an enclosure of surprise and intrigue. The small world created here has the power to highlight aspects of how we sense and make sense of the wider environment in general, quite apart from the field of meaning and symbolism. At the same time, it is singularly appropriate that a city infused with mystery and illusion should include a sculptural trompe l'œil within its repertoire.

The first glimpse of the sculpture gives no indication of what is in store. Approaching nearer the work, it is evident that, although the outside of the trunks are untouched, apart from removal of the bark, glimpses of the inward-facing sides reveal low-relief carving. Once inside the enclosure the detailed sculpturing on parts of each individual trunk is evident, although closer examination does not provide coherence. This is achieved from one position only: from a seat hollowed out in the thirteenth elm at one end of the enclosure. Here, at the origin of the perspective, the scene composes before the observer: a classically-proportioned room with evidence of a meal - a table set with a basket of loaves, pitcher of wine, bowls and cups. The architectural symmetry is all the more surprising, given the variation in thickness, height and shape of the trunks forming the enclosure. They are far from identical columns. As a trompe l'oeil achieved through sculptural perspective, the scene disintegrates the moment the observer leaves the seat.

Laboratory

The common initial reaction to the experience of The Upper Room is one of surprise, wonder, amazement. This is followed by curiosity, as the observer puzzles how the artist conceived and executed a sculpture to deceive the eye. Hence, the enclosed space can take on the character of a laboratory, a place in which to linger, to analyse and examine, in an attempt to satisfy our curiosity. One is therefore drawn to explore the nature of vision and perception - both how the eye composes and is deceived - in relation to the geometry of perspective, ahead of any reflection on place meaning.

The Upper Room, then, is a modern example of the illusionistic technique which followed the 'invention' of linear perspective by Western art in the 15th century,[1] and which is most commonly associated with the vaulted and domed ceilings of particular churches of the 16th and 17th centuries, where the optical effect is achieved by a combination of sculptural form and colour. Here, from the viewing position, the side walls appear solid. (Although, if the sun is shining, for much of the day the cross-shadows cast by the columns on the floor of wood·chippings expose the illusion, and show the spaces to be twice the width of the trunks they separate). The end wall is formed from three trunks which are thinly separated towards the upper level. Each of the gaps narrows if one eye in turn is closed, or disappears with a slight move of the head. - This is the clearest illustration of several to warn against equating the optics of the camera's lens to that of our binocular vision.

Aloft, the room is open to the sky, or, rather, to the green foliage of trees among which the sculpture stands, a feature of which one is aware from the first sight of the work. A cross-beamed ceiling to the room is, however, indicated to varying extent at the tops of the individual columns. Interestingly, such carving may be sufficient for the ceiling to 'compose' for the seated observer. Theoretically, this would certainly occur - and the ceiling appear complete - given a normal 'cone of vision' directed straight ahead at the acknowledged angle of 15 degrees below the horizontal for a seated person.[2] The eye, let alone the head, is, however, never still. As a result, not only is the ceiling 'breached', but much more in general is assumed to be in view than is in fact possible at any one moment. The ever-scanning eye overcomes its concentrated focus in the service of the naturally inquisitive onlooker. "What would vision be without eye movement?" mused Merleau-Ponty.[3] In terms of scientific measurement, the answer would be that the stationary eye has a focus of detailed recognition restricted to a cone subtended at an angle of a mere 10 degrees to a central 'bulls-eye' of vision, the limit of symbol recognition is no more than about 30 degrees, and colour discrimination, 60 degrees, in a general all-round lateral 'awareness' which extends to some 180 degrees.

Research would also expose our assumed (square or rectangular) 'frame' of vision. The very sunken position of our eyes means that our window-on-the-world cannot. resemble the standard frame of painting, photograph, film or television screen through which we are continually viewing other worlds. Rather, it is oval in shape. Such detail, however, rarely surfaces - it would require conscious experimental direction to detect - since any important peripheral restriction of vision is automatically overcome by movement of the head.

Figures 52-54 illustrate the different stages of a visual engagement with the sculpture. The approach to the collection of tree trunks is followed by the composed photograph, with a field of view corresponding to that of the eye focusing straight ahead. (When, as here, the object visible through the viewfinder is identical in size and distance to what is seen by the human eye, the (zoom) lens of a 35mm camera registers a focal length of 65mm. The horizontal viewing angle at this focal length measures 30 degrees – a figure corresponding to the limit of symbol recognition mentioned above). The full extent of visual awareness, with its rapid outward decline in acuity, is suggested in the third illustration. It assumes no movement of head or eye, which, although perhaps unexpected and considered unrealistic, nevertheless represents the momentary reality. The reaction of persons in the viewing chair may be taken as confirming this general process, for, after initial comment on the sudden coherence of the work, reference is made

Fig. 52 Approach to the Upper Room sculpture.

Fig. 53 The Upper Room, camera's eye.

to a succession of particular details - items on the table, beamed ceiling, views through particular windows, a money bag, and so on. Several of these items reflect careful observation on what would be at the periphery, and thus beyond recognition, of a forward-directed vision.

Fig. 54 The Upper Room, human eye.

The Upper Room, in being designed to arouse curiosity, thereby invites extended investigation of the kind discussed above. In so doing, it shows perception to be active, not passive, and can be used to illustrate the general parameters of vision and the crucial role of eye movement. The eye composes by sensing and making sense of what is before it. In the world beyond, no less than in this laboratory, a composition or view or scene only holds true from one position. Change, even disappearance, is the norm. As a trompe l'oeil, the sculpture also dramatically illustrates how the eye can be deceived, a feature we are perhaps reluctant to accept in our general lives, where the 'eye-witness' is accorded special credence.

Place

When curiosity yields to acceptance and perception turns to reflection, then The Upper Room is no longer a laboratory, space to explore, but a place of significance and meaning. Separation is a key quality in the emergence and recognition of place. Here, the sculpture is dramatically bounded and set apart. Externally, the upright trunks are rough, untouched; internally the trunks are smooth, ordered and finely carved. Gothic greenery contrasts with classical symmetry. Externally, the appearance may bring to mind a prehistoric monument of standing stones; internally, the individual wooden columns carry echoes of a cathedral's stone column-work. (Both metaphors suggest holy ground: being set apart is a quality of holiness). The bounded nature and separation combine for the observer in the carved seat to confirm the experience of insideness, as opposed to outsideness. Inside is culture, outside is nature.

The name affirms its being. The Upper Room announces the setting for one of humankind's significant happenings. Thirteen elms represent the number of persons involved, but no personage is represented. (It is not called, The Last Supper). The observer is alone. We therefore, not only compose the scene visually, but also recreate and interact with the Christian iconography to experience the immanence of a holy place. (It is probable that a majority arrive in a particular frame of mind, having also made, or about to make, a pilgrimage to the cathedral a mere 300 metres away). The privileged participant is permanently about to break into history. The event of which The Upper Room is the setting - the gathering of his followers by the Saviour presaging his own death and rising again - is symbolised here in the bringing together of scattered trunks and giving new life to the dead elms. Place always gathers.

The human role in defining place, then, is emphasized in this present instance. There is no company: the lone observer is sat back into a seat hewn out of a trunk, the sides of which restrict vision. The outside world is excluded. It is in such confinement that the divine in nature may be found, the present instance being a clear example in the English Romantic tradition, even though the impulse here may not be of a vernal wood. It is the clearly-recognisable iconography, however, which induces an interpretation of the room as a particular holy place. It is therefore appropriate that such a reading engages the dialectic between faith and certainty, sight and knowledge, stability and instability, life and death.

Concluding comments

The Upper Room is an intriguing sculpture. As a modern piece of public art, it is not designed to advertise or help foster regeneration of city or region. There is no political motive. It is the gift of cathedral authorities and the work of an artist with a free commission. As a work of art, it has trickery at its core, but owes nothing to the playfulness of postmodernism. It is a novel exploitation of the 15th century discovery of perspective. In so doing, it illustrates the twin nature of human experience - of head and heart, of perception and reflection, reason and imagination. Constructed as a trompe l'œil, it invites exploration of the working of the human eye and the nature of vision. Having accepted the perspective of space, then place emerges existentially, guided by its religious iconography.

Finally, in the context of Durham, the sculpture is an embodiment of one's experience of the city, standing as it does in the centre of a city infused with illusion. Deception begins with the sudden and dramatic entry. The drama, with greenery present until the last moment, is born of a few channelled traverses of the rolling, winding topography amid what a map will show to be a ragged disposition of town and country.

The massive cathedral, justifying the appellation city, suggests it surely presides over a metropolis, not a modest county town. Views from the riverside give a towering significance to the peninsula's buildings, domestic as well as monumental. The weirs, ponding back the flow of water, inflate the stature of the river. (Without the weirs, past defence would have been weakened, and present boating impossible. An occasional bird, its feet awash as it perches on the weir between the two former mills, is an immediate measure of the meagre flow). Meanwhile, the greenery of the River Banks evinces a natural scene in what in reality is a manicured landscape where every tree has been planted and nurtured. The accompanying imagined tranquillity also obscures the proximate urban cacophony, unless the dominance of the eye over ear is intentionally challenged. How appropriate, therefore, that at the very heart of this scene, an artist should choose to add his own sculptural illusion.

References

Chapter 1

1. Walter Scott, 'Harold the Dauntless' in *The Poetical Works of Sir Walter Scott*, Frederick Warne: London (1897), 320.
2. Philip Larkin, *Collected Poems*, Faber & Faber Ltd: London (1988).
3. T.S. Eliot, *Collected Poems*, Faber & Faber Ltd: London (1963).

Chapter 2

1. R. Hamer, *A Choice of Anglo-Saxon Verse*, Faber & Faber: London (1970), 33.
2. R.J. Dickinson 'A description of Durham by Laurence the Monk', in R.J. Dickinson (ed) *City of Durham, 1179-1979*, Guinness & Rawson, Newcastle (1979), 12.
3. L.T. Smith (ed) *The Itinerary of John Leland*, Jonathan Cape: London, part 1, 73.
4. C. Morris (ed) *The Journeys of Celia Fiennes*, Gresset: London (1949), 213
5. P. Rogers (ed) *Daniel Defoe: A Tour through the Whole Kingdom of Great Britain*, Penguin: Harmondsworth (1971), 533.
6. Robert Hegge, *The Legend of St. Cuthbert*, George Smith: Darlington (1777), 22.
7. Quoted in D. Pocock and R. Gazzard, *Durham: Portrait of a Cathedral City*, City of Durham Trust and Dept. of Geography, Durham (1983), 26.
8. James Murray, *The Travels of the Imagination: A True Journey from Newcastle to London*, W. Fordyce: Newcastle (1828), 34.
9. L.M. Knapp (ed), *Tobias Smollett: The Expedition of Humphrey Clinker*, Oxford University Press: Oxford (1966), 187.
10. R.W. Chapman (ed) *The Letters of Samuel Johnson*, Clarendon Press: Oxford (1952), vol. 1, 339.
11. W.M. Hutchinson, *The History and Antiquities of the County Palatine of Durham*, Newcastle (1787), vol 2., 1-2.
12. J.B. Priestley, *English Journey*, Penguin: Harmondsworth (1977), 302.
13. William Conton, *The African*, Heinemann: London (1960), 48.
14. James Kirkup, *The Submerged Village and Other Poems*, Oxford University Press: London (1951), 59.
15. Tony Harrison, *From the School of Eloquence and Other Poems*, Rex Collings: London (1978), 34.
16. G.W.E. Russell (ed), *Letters of Matthew Arnold*, Macmillan: London (1895), vol. 1, 154.
17. R. Stewart (ed), *National Hawthorne, The English Notebooks*, George Bell & Sons: London (1941), 543.
18. T. Gray, 'Letter to Rev. Mr. Brown, 24th July 1753, in P. Toynbee and L. Whibley, *Correspondence of Thomas Gray*, Oxford University Press: Oxford (1935) vol 1, 379-80.
19. T. Sharp, *op. cit.*, 41.
20. William Conton, *op. cit.*, 49.

Chapter 3

1. S. Cantacuzino, 'Durham is distinctive and of international importance' in J. Crosby and D. Pocock (eds) *Durham: A City in Trust*, City of Durham Trust, Durham (1993), 17-21.
2. A Clifton-Taylor, *Another Six English Towns*, BBC: London (1984), 175-205.
3. W. Whitfield, 'Visions of Durham, IV' in D. Pocock (ed) *Visions of Durham*, City of Durham Trust, Durham (1990), 34-39.
4. N. Pevsner (revised E. Williamson) *The Buildings of England: County Durham*, Penguin: Harmondsworth (1983), 159-60.
5. *The Times*, 14th July 1944.
6. City of Durham District, *Historic Environment Handbook*, Durham (1999).

7. D. Pocock and R. Gazzard, *op. cit.*, 44-65.
8. M. Roberts, *Book of Durham*, Batsford/English Heritage, London (1994).

Chapter 4

1. The resident population was tapped by a systematic sample of one hundred persons from the electoral roll; 94 questionnaires were completed. Visitors were tapped via one in ten callers at the City's information bureau in July and August; 59 of the 190 forms were returned. Both took place in 1973.
2. Thomas Sharp, *Town and Townscape*, John Murray: London (1968), 73.

Chapter 6

1. Anon., 'The world's best buildings,' part I, *The Illustrated London News* (May 1984) 50-57.
2. Bill Bryson, *Notes from a Small Island*, Black Swan: London (1996), 295.
3. N. Pevsner, *Outline of European Architecture*, Penguin: Harmondsworth (1963), 66.
4. A Clifton-Taylor, *Another Six English Towns*, BBC: London (1984), 181.
5. G. Zarnecki, J. Holt, T. Holland (eds), *English Romanesque Art, 1066-1200*, G. Weidenfeld & Nicolson Ltd.: London (1984).
6. T.G. Jackson, *op. cit.*, 223.
7. D. Pocock and R. Gazzard, *op. cit.*, 25-43.
8. N. Pevsner (revised by E. Williamson), *op. cit.*, 159-60.
9. Quoted in Pocock and Gazzard, *op. cit.*, 26.
10. F.H. Rushford, *City Beautiful: A vision of Durham*, County Advertiser: Durham (1944).
11. G.M. Trevelyan, *History of England*, Longmans: London (1926), 120.
12. Walter Scott, *op. cit.*, 320.
13. *The Times*, 14th July 1944.
14. T. Sharp, *op. cit.*, 88-89.
15. *Durham Advertiser*, 21st July 1944.
16. *Northern Echo*, 15th July 1944.
17. Durham County Council, *Durham Cathedral: Artists and Images*, Durham County Council, Durham (1993), 43-48.

Chapter 8

1. J.M.W. Turner *Picturesque Views in England and Wales* (1827-38). See Eric Shanes, *Turner's Picturesque Views in England and Wales* (1979) Chatto and Windus: London.
2. Fieldwork was conducted between 10.30-12.45 and 14.00-16.45 on July 14, 16, 21-25, August 26-28, 1980.
3. M.J. Friedländer, *Landscape Portrait, Still Life: The Origin and Development*, Oxford University Press: Oxford (1949), 121.
4. C. Day Lewis, *The Poetic Image*, Jonathan Cape: London (1947) 24.

Chapter 9

1. E.H. Gombrich, *Art and Illusion*, Phaidon: London (1960).
2. H. Dreyfus, *The Measure of Man: Human Factors in Design*, Whitney Publications: New York (1959).
3. M. Merleau-Ponty, 'Eye and Mind' in G.A. Johnson and M.B. Smith (eds) *The Merleau-Ponty Aesthetics Reader*, Northwestern University Press: Evanston (1993), 124.